ABOUT CANADA

Women's Rights

Women's Rights

PENNI MITCHELL

FERNWOOD
PUBLISHING

HALIFAX & WINNIPEG

Editing: Jessica Antony
Design: John van der Woude
Printed and bound in Canada

Published in Canada by Fernwood Publishing
32 Oceanvista Lane, Black Point, Nova Scotia, B0J 1B0
and 748 Broadway Avenue, Winnipeg, MB R3G 0X3
www.fernwoodpublishing.ca

Fernwood Publishing Company Limited gratefully acknowledges the financial support of the Government of Canada through the Canada Book Fund and the Canada Council for the Arts, the Nova Scotia Department of Communities, Culture and Heritage, the Manitoba Department of Culture, Heritage and Tourism under the Manitoba Publishers Marketing Assistance Program and the Province of Manitoba, through the Book Publishing Tax Credit, for our publishing program.

Library and Archives Canada Cataloguing in Publication

Mitchell, Penni, 1959-, author
About Canada : women's rights / Penni Mitchell.

(About Canada series)
Includes index.
Issued in print and electronic formats.
ISBN 978-1-55266-737-8 (pbk.).--ISBN 978-1-55266-750-7 (epub)

1. Women--Canada--History. 2. Women's rights--Canada--History. I. Title.
II. Title: Women's rights. III. Series: About Canada series

HQ1453.M58 2015   305.40971   C2015-900669-4
C2015-900670-8

CONTENTS

FROM BLUESTOCKINGS
TO BRA-BURNERS

Women in Canada have participated in wars, panned for gold and risked their lives to help fugitive slaves. At times, women dressed as men to gain entry into jobs prohibited to them and they also donned white gloves before chaining themselves to Canada's Parliamentary Gallery.

Women also led successful campaigns for government-paid hospitals, for the pasteurization of milk, for the vote and for child protection laws. Women's collective efforts led to Canada's first minimum wage laws, mothers' allowance programs, birth control clinics and a treaty to ban nuclear testing.

In spite of these achievements, however, few women in Canada are celebrated as nation builders.

And yet, by the time of the colonization of the continent — known by its original inhabitants as Turtle Island — women in many Aboriginal societies were already reputed as nation builders. Aboriginal women often influenced matters of state and negotiated peace accords between nations. Aboriginal women, including Métis women, were also integral to the early fur trade; they worked as translators and brokered trade agreements. In New France, colonial women set up the first schools and hospitals, and were among the colony's first administrators.

Black women led efforts to help fleeing slaves settle in Canada and were also among the first publishers of abolitionist (anti-slavery) newspapers in Canada West (now Ontario). In early Black communities, women organized the pooling of money to help those in need. In fact, programs like unemployment insurance can trace their roots to benevolent societies organized by women.

Canada's history is filled with brave women who stepped out of the rigid confines of gender expectations to participate as equal citizens in public life. Yet attempts to squelch their ambitions met them at every turn. The first female physicians in Canada trained with the intention of providing medical care to women, children and the underprivileged; they often provided medical care at no cost. However, women first had to fight tooth and nail to force Canadian universities to accept female medical students. Male students revolted when women were first admitted, and early female students were sexually harassed.

For more than one hundred years, women stubbornly chipped away at the pantheon of laws that gave husbands control over their wives and children, and fought against laws that reserved the rights and privileges of citizenship for certain classes and races of men. Women forced opened doors not only to universities, but judges' chambers, police academies, the RCMP and the prime minister's residence.

The first recorded resistance of women in Canada took place in the early colonial beginnings of New France. In December 1757, Montreal women marched to the residence of Governor Pierre de Rigaud de Vaudreuil to protest his decision to end the distribution of bread during the Seven Years' War. Quebec women later succeeded after a second protest involving four hundred women took place in 1759.

Interestingly, women also took to the streets to protest wartime bread rations and to demand price controls to control wartime inflation during the French Revolution. It was at this time that a woman in France named Olympe de Gouges published the first women's rights treatise. In 1791, de Gouges produced *Déclaration des Droits de la Femme et de la Citoyenne*. Her declaration called for full equal rights for women under law, within marriage and in society at large, including the right to vote and to serve as legislators and magistrates. Her manifesto followed the adoption of the *Declaration of the Rights of Man and of the Citizen* by France's National Constituent Assembly. It was de Gouges' belief that since women could be guillotined on an equal basis as men, women were entitled to a say in their governance. The French national assembly responded by banning women's clubs, and de Gouges, a playwright, was sent to the gallows in November 1793. A report of her execution in a French journal stated: "The law has punished this conspirator for having forgotten the virtues that belong to her sex."[1]

The idea that women should not step outside their proscribed role as subordinates was not unique to France or New France. In British women's salons, reformers called bluestockings advanced the idea that women were men's moral and intellectual equals — a radical idea rejected by influential English thinkers like Jean Jacques Rousseau. Nonetheless, female Enlightenment proponents of the eighteenth century used reason to advance their views, and bluestockings reasoned that education for girls would improve women's lot in life.

Bluestocking societies were made up of women (and some men) of the middle classes. It could scarcely have been otherwise since women of the lower classes generally could not read, let alone pen articles arguing for the need for their education. One bluestocking writer, identified as "Maria," painstakingly set out the cause for girls' education in a January 23, 1782, letter in the *Gazetteer and New Daily Advertiser* in London. "If it be allowed that the principles of virtue and vice are the same in both sexes," Maria wrote, "I think there should be an equal attention paid to the forming of the minds of one as the other." Maria went on to encourage well-to-do ladies to "pay as much attention to adorn their minds as they do their persons."[2]

Much like the term "bra-burner" is thought of, "bluestocking" was a diminutive label that suggested a low station in life. Blue stockings were the common worsted stockings worn in Europe in the eighteenth century, while black stockings made from dyed silk were worn by the

This nineteenth-century cartoon, published in Britain's Punch *magazine, satirized the Rational Dress Movement, which sought less restrictive clothing for women.*

more affluent. Although the name was intended as a slight, women embraced the term and claimed it as their own.

At the same time that Olympe de Gouges was protesting with the Society of Revolutionary Republican Women in France, Mary Wollstonecraft was writing *A Vindication of the Rights of Woman*, published in 1792. Wollstonecraft radically argued that women should participate in all aspects of public life. She eloquently challenged the prevailing notion that women were naturally inferior to men. And, like Maria, she took swipes at the rich. "The education of the rich tends to render them vain and helpless," Wollstonecraft wrote. "They only live to amuse themselves."[3] For her efforts, Wollstonecraft was routinely castigated in the press as a "hyena in petticoats."

The more women pushed, the more their opponents attacked their gender attributes in an effort to misrepresent their cause. In the later 1800s, American suffragist and abolitionist Susan B. Anthony was regularly referred to as a "man-hater." When women protested oppressive corsets and restrictive clothing, they were harassed on the streets for wearing the pantaloon garment advocated by newspaperwoman Amelia Bloomer. A generation later in Britain, suffragists were stereotyped as tea-totalling socialites sheltered by upper-class privilege. And yet, Emmeline Pankhurst and those who gathered under the Women's Social and Political

Mary Wollstonecraft wrote Vindication of the Rights of Woman *in 1792.*

Union banner were clobbered in London streets by police and thrown in jail, bloodied. Undaunted by the gropings and the obscenities hurled at them on Britain's streets, they burned the words "Votes for Women" in acid on the putting greens of an exclusive golf course in 1913. Inspired by factory workers' radicalism, suffragettes went on hunger strikes in jail where they were violently force-fed by prison staff, a painful procedure that involved pushing a tube down their throats, often causing injury.[4]

Early suffragists in Canada were cast as homewreckers and neglectful mothers by opponents on the political right and left. Many male trade unionists believed that women's efforts to improve pay for female factory workers undermined male workers' entitlement to a "family wage." Similarly, women in the West who fought for rights such as the reinstatement of dower rights — an entitlement to a one-third stake in property following the death of a spouse — were cast as bourgeoisie.

The counter-attacks resurfaced fifty years later during the women's liberation era. It started when feminists in Atlantic City, New Jersey, held a protest at the 1968 Miss America beauty pageant. The demonstration included a "freedom trash can" into which symbols of women's subjugation were placed, including girdles, false eyelashes and *Cosmopolitan* magazine. The protest aimed to challenge the narrow beauty standards that contributed to the subordination of women as sex objects. However, no bras were burned in the freedom trash can and its contents weren't set ablaze because event organizers didn't obtain a fire permit. Nonetheless, feminists soon were labelled "bra-burners" and the term became emblematic of unruly women at a time when draft cards were burned at anti-Vietnam War protests.

Whether they fought to improve the lot of working-class women, married women, jailed women, slaves, enlisted women, Aboriginal women, unmarried mothers or battered women, feminists have been criticized less for their ideals than for their refusal to abide by society's gendered expectations. Stereotypes have also reinforced a skewed view of women's history, one in which feminists' accomplishments and motives are often miscast or misunderstood. From bluestockings to bra-burners, women who have demanded equal rights have been dismissed as unattractive heretics (hairy-legged feminists) or self-interested and frivolous (white, middle-class housewives). It is a feminist paradox that many women who succeeded in fighting gender discrimination were judged to be failures as women. Still today, women who step onto the public stage are measured according to their adherence to strict beauty standards, on the basis of their desirability to men, their function as wives or mothers or on the basis of the perceived limitations of their class or race attributes.

While it is accurate that many female reformers came from middle- or upper-class backgrounds, it is also true that many of the measures feminists fought for over the last century — from female factory inspectors to equal pay — bridged class boundaries. Early women reformers were generally no more privileged than male reformers such as J.S. Woodsworth and Tommy Douglas. In fact, influential male political reformers, from Karl Marx and Mahatma Ghandi, to Martin Luther King Jr. and Nelson Mandela, were all educated men from privileged families. In each case, however, they came to be regarded as heroes who used their privileged status to help mobilize others and to demand greater rights for oppressed people.

Following the First International Women's Conference in Paris in 1892, the term feminist, from the French word féministe, began to be used in English to refer to the advocacy of equal rights for women. Just as male reformers mobilized for change, feminists realized that joining forces with others was the way forward. It was clear that in order to affect the changes they sought, women would need equal civil rights, including not only the vote, but the right to hold public office — just for starters. Later, they would ensure future generations of women would have the right to equal pay, to control their fertility, to keep their Indian status and to have equal rights as minority groups enshrined in the Canadian Charter of Rights and Freedoms.

More than a hundred years ago, while still prohibited from voting or running for political office, women gained a political voice through farm, labour, temperance and women's benevolent clubs. They coalesced around the idea that society should take care of its citizens. A national system of pensions was needed to avert poverty in old age; a system of public welfare was needed to minimize the poverty of widows and deserted mothers; labour laws were needed to protect vulnerable female and children labourers; minimum wage laws were needed to ensure girls and women were paid above slave wages; and public hospitals paid from tax dollars were essential for the well-being of all.

It is important to note, however, that while those who carried the banner of women's rights shared common aims, they also had many differences. They did not all share the same ethnicity, class or political affiliation, for example. They shared common goals but often had different philosophies. Some early reformers held that female suffrage (the right to vote) would pave the way for the prohibition of alcohol, which they believed caused men to squander their paycheques and beat their wives. Many female factory workers didn't support a ban on alcohol but saw the vote as a means to better their working conditions. Meanwhile, some reformers argued that women's sphere in the home made them uniquely suited to public life; they held that the values of nurturing and caring for others should be expanded into the public sphere. Others believed women should be allowed into male arenas, including the military, as a matter of fairness. Many reformers viewed minimum wage laws as a means to guarantee a minimal level of earnings for women, but some viewed "protectionist" laws as patronizing. And when five Alberta feminists fought for the appointment of women to the Senate in the Person's Case, some of their sisters in the Western farm movement scoffed and said it would be better to abolish the Senate.

While their divergent views often confounded outsiders, and at times caused dissent among insiders, it can also be argued that it has been the diversity of those who championed women's rights that has enabled feminism to adapt, transform and redefine itself in each generation.

It is my hope that this book will help increase awareness of the pivotal roles women have played in Canada's story. For too long, women have been relegated to the margins of history, creating a skewed view of both men's and women's roles in Canada's history and its development. Furthermore, learning about how women were key figures throughout history builds a sense of pride in the accomplishments of our foremothers.

My intent is to illuminate the determined efforts of just some of the women who climbed on soapboxes and defied the limitations assigned to their gender. In so doing, these women helped build a more caring and just nation. The visionary thinking of women has changed our notions about human rights, equality and gender, the responsibility of government and the meaning of justice. Women's collective efforts have led to improvements in the lives of women and children, as well as helped achieve greater freedoms for racial and religious minorities, people with disabilities and LGBTQ Canadians.

The 150-year-long fight by women for equality, fairness and

Sexism In the City The best & worst cities to be a woman in Canada

BEST			
1 / QUÉBEC CITY	6 / TORONTO	11 / REGINA	16 / KITCHENER-CAMBRIDGE-WATERLOO
2 / SASKATOON	7 / OTTAWA-GATINEAU	12 / WINNIPEG	17 / CALGARY
3 / ST. JOHN'S	8 / SHERBROOKE	13 / VANCOUVER	18 / WINDSOR
4 / MONTREAL	9 / HALIFAX	14 / ST. CATHARINES	19 / OSHAWA
5 / VICTORIA	10 / HAMILTON	15 / LONDON	20 / EDMONTON

WORST

policyalternatives.ca/best-worst

A 2014 CCPA study by Kate McInturf revealed the best and worst places to be a woman in Canada. It ranked Canada's twenty largest metropolitan areas based on a comparison of how men and women are faring in five areas: economic security, leadership, health, personal security and education.
Credit: Canadian Centre for Policy Alternatives <https://www.policyalternatives.ca/best-worst#sthash.CTvmZLEl.dpuf>

justice is an integral part of Canada's social history, just as the history of Aboriginal peoples, the history of slavery and the history of colonialism are formative to Canada's creation. I am not a historian, but a journalist. My exploration into the history of women's rights therefore relied upon many indepth books written by historians, and I encourage readers to consult the books referenced in the endnotes for a more thorough examination of the topics in this book. I am grateful to have had the opportunity to write about some of the women who broke down barriers to create a more just and fair society. They have inspired me and I hope their actions inspire readers to continue to work to make Canada a more just and fair country. Much remains to be done.

FIRST NATIONS WOMEN

Though each First Nation has a distinct history and unique cultural traditions, women in many Aboriginal societies held positions of influence that were greater than those held by most women in European or settler societies. Women in many First Nations were known as skilled negotiators of tribal disputes. The views of clan mothers commonly held sway and women's roles were often complementary to those of men. As writer-researcher Randi Cull describes, "Aboriginal people had a well-established system of governance and a complex social structure ... the pre-contact Aboriginal social structure was for the most part matrilineal. This was in sharp contrast to the established European patriarchal norms."[1]

Thus, through legislative and other controls, the process of colonization not only stripped all Aboriginal people of their lands, cultural practices, laws, spirituality and independence, but it undermined the status of Aboriginal women in specific and gendered ways.

Anishinaabe women "had authority and power within our societies that was equal to that of men," writes Patricia D. McGuire, co-editor of *First Voices: An Aboriginal Women's Reader*. It was common for women in many First Nations to perform sacred rites. As well, religious or spiritual beliefs were not traditionally used to keep women subordinate, as they were in Christian societies. In one Anishinaabe creation story, McGuire recalls how "water was given to the women to care for because only women have the ability to create water and sustain life within our bodies."[2]

Many Aboriginal women were involved in governance. In her article, "Women in Iroquois Society," Cyndy Baskin, a professor in the School of Social Work at Ryerson University, describes how Iroquois "women often addressed councils; their opinion was asked and heeded … by their authority as owners of the land and their concern for the future of their children, they took an active part in telling sachems (chiefs) what to do."[3] Haudenosaunee women (Iroquois), writes historian Jan Noel, were "the authorities over the longhouses, children, marriages and slaves."[4]

Among Okanogan First Nations, writes Okanogan author and educator Jeannette Armstrong, "it was traditionally the women who made decisions about resources, who made decisions about the land, who made decisions about the wealth, and who carefully constructed a balance of power in the family."[5]

An Iroquois woman acting in an official capacity was known as a *gantowisa*. Gantowisas ran local clan councils, according to Barbara Alice Mann in *Iroquoian Women: The Gantowisas*. "They held all the lineage wampum, nomination belts and titles … They nominated all male sachems as well as all clan mothers to office … They appointed warriors, declared war, negotiated peace and mediated disputes."[6]

WOMEN AND THE FUR TRADE

Aboriginal women were actively involved in the trade between Aboriginal trappers and European traders that grew in the seventeenth century. Aboriginal women often accompanied men on animal hunting expeditions; they cleaned pelts and prepared them for market. This labour-intensive work determined, to a great extent, the quality of the pelt and therefore its price. Aboriginal women also participated in the fur trade as guides, interpreters, cooks, canoe builders and clothing makers. Many were also skilled trappers; Cree grandmothers taught hunting and trapping to children.

The involvement of Aboriginal women as negotiators was noted in the records of traders, company administrators and missionaries. Women described in these records were often those whose services were used by fur traders or military forces. York Factory trading post records indicate that one such woman was Thanadelthur, a young Dene woman who lived in what is now northern Manitoba.

In 1713, Thanadelthur was taken captive during a raid by Cree on her community. She escaped along the Nelson River a year later and, after a difficult journey, met a group of Hudson's Bay Company hunters and travelled with them to York Factory. Thanadelthur, who spoke three languages, discussed the untapped resources of the area with Hudson Bay Company governor James Knight. Knight sought to increase trade with the Dene, but there was a long-standing animosity between them and the Cree, York Factory's main fur suppliers. Thanadelthur went

Thanadelthur was a Dene woman who served as a peacemaker and intermediary among traders at Fork York.
Illustration: Amanda Dow from children's book Blackships/Thanadelthur *published by Heartland Associates.*

on to serve as a negotiator on a peace mission that was a three-way negotiation between 150 people that included representatives of the Dene, Cree and Hudson's Bay Company. She is credited with brokering the difficult but important May 1716 peace accord that helped the company expand trade to the Churchill River Post the next year.[7]

Further east, in the central Great Lakes region in 1790, an Aboriginal woman named Netnokwa "was regarded as principal chief of the Ottawwaws," according to Mona Holmlund and Gail Youngberg, authors of *Inspiring Women: A Celebration of Herstory*. "Netnokwa had lost a son and subsequently purchased John Tanner, a white captive boy of about 12, to replace him." Tanner, who was later re-united with his birth family, wrote of his adoptive mother, "She could accomplish whatever she pleased, either with the traders or the Indians; probably in some measure, because she never attempted to do anything which was not right or just."[8]

On the west coast, too, First Nations women were reputed for their trading skills. Captain James Strange, who was in charge of a British trade vessel seeking sea otter pelts, recorded his observances of Nootka women in what is now British Columbia. He wrote in his journal: "I dreaded the sight of a woman, for whenever any were present, they were sure to preside over and direct all commercial transactions, and as that was the case, I was obliged to pay three times the price for what in their absence, I could have procured for one third of the value."[9]

Another sign of Nootka women's status was observed by Strange when the fur traders tried, unsuccessfully, to pay Nootka men for sexual services from Nootka women. According to University of British Columbia history professor Jean Barman in *Indigenous Women and Feminism: Politics, Activism, Culture*, Nootka men did not have sexual control over Nootka women. "Women at Nootka are highly esteemed and treated with as much tenderness, as in the most civilized countries of Europe," Strange unselfconsciously observed.[10]

During the fur trade era, many Aboriginal women entered into long-term relationships with European fur traders and company administrators. Some became legally married but most unions were informal "country marriages." In spite of the skills and knowledge Aboriginal women brought to trading posts and settlements, many country wives were abandoned by European men when they no longer served their needs. Among them was Margaret Taylor, a Métis woman who, in 1826, entered a country marriage with George Simpson, Governor of Rupert's Land. Simpson, who had earlier had children with another country wife, abandoned Taylor and their two sons four years later to marry his eighteen-year-old cousin from England.

Marriages between European men and Aboriginal women were officially discouraged by the Hudson's Bay Company. Mixed race liaisons were more commonly encouraged by the North West Company because they were considered good for trade business. Fort Langley, B.C., records from the Hudson's Bay trading post indicate that supervisors informally encouraged young men in the second year of their three-year employment contracts to "take a woman" on a more or less permanent basis. In doing so, Jean Barman recounts in *Indigenous Feminism*, employees were more likely to renew their work contracts.[11]

Indigenous women sometimes had little choice who they worked for. In Labrador, a young Inuit woman named Mikak was kidnapped in 1767 after her husband was killed by members of a military detachment from Fort York in Chateau Bay. Her captors, impressed by her skills and keen mind, sent Mikak to school in England and, when she returned, she became a negotiator between the British and the Inuit.[12]

Molly Brant was a leader who helped broker Mohawk support for the British.
Credit: Illustration created by Sara Tyson.

At around the same time, Mohawk Molly Brant (Konwatsi' tsiaienni) and William Johnson, British Superintendent of Indian Affairs, were a formidable couple in the New York region. Brant's influence within her Mohawk clan, one of the six members of the powerful Iroquois Confederacy, was significant. Brant was able to direct wartime conduct of young warriors[13] and she played a pivotal role in the U.S. Revolutionary War after William Johnson's death. When the war broke out in 1775, Brant used her influence to secure Iroquois support for the British. She sent runners to the British commander to warn of a planned attack on Fort Stanwix by American forces in 1777. Commander Alexander Fraser ranked Brant's influence "far superior to that of all their Chiefs put together."

Following the war, British officials arranged for Brant and her family, which included eight children, to move to Fort Niagara on Lake Ontario. She settled near Kingston, received a British pension and was an influential member of the community. In 1996, the city of Kingston proclaimed August 25 as Molly Brant Celebration Day.

WOMEN AND THE INDIAN ACT

After the British gained control of New France in 1791, they imposed greater control over First Nations people and lands through treaties and other means. Later, as the fur trade declined, Aboriginal people became less valuable to colonists.

Under the Constitution Act, 1867 (originally the British North America Act), Canada's legislators imposed a system whereby legislative control of Indians and lands reserved for Indians was assigned to the federal government. The Indian Act of 1876 further entrenched the domination of Aboriginal peoples under Canada's laws and, at the same time, imposed gender domination over Aboriginal women by Aboriginal men. As a direct result, women were stripped of many traditional roles that involved decision making and they were prohibited from participating in band meetings. The Indian Act and a host of related regulations also forbade cultural ceremonies that reinforced many First Nations social values.[14]

The Dominion government further imposed a European-style system of male domination through marriage laws, property ownership rules and the imposition of Christianity. The Indian Act created a hierarchy of Indianness that distinguished between Métis, or mixed ancestry people, Indians living on reserves, non-status Indians and Inuit. The distinctions discriminated against women and weakened Aboriginal societies further. For example, many First Nations were matrilineal cultures in which lineage was transferred on the mother's side. But the federal government defined Indian identity as a status transferred only by male parentage.

Predominant among the gendered controls was the stipulation that women who married non-Indian men would lose any benefits they held as Indians. Furthermore, any children born of such unions would not receive benefits. Women who married non-status Indians were often banished from their communities and their family ties were often severed. Indian men who married non-Indians not only continued to maintain rights as Indians, but their wives and children gained Indian status.[15]

Another serious blow to the social fabric of First Nations came when potlatch ceremonies, common among west coast First Nations, were criminalized from 1884 to 1951. Potlatch ceremonies involved spirit dances and theatre and were held to mark a birth, marriage, adoption, death or other event. They were an important economic and cultural practice that involved redistributing community wealth. Goods such as blankets, horses, food and canoes were bestowed with great ceremony. Missionaries cited the potlatch as an impediment to assimilation because the ceremonies stabilized clan relations. According to the *Canadian Encyclopedia*, "By the time the ban was repealed in 1951, serious damage had been caused to tribal identities and social stratification."[16]

By imposing a system of restrictive laws upon First Nations that, on the one hand, embedded a gendered system of power upon their communities, and usurped lands, customs, language and freedoms on the other, the communal underpinnings of First Nations were severely weakened.

Aboriginal women suffered in distinct ways. In her book *The Importance of Being Monogamous: Marriage and Nation Building in Western Canada to 1915*, Sarah Carter notes that many First Nations customs permitted divorce and remarriage. "The ease with which divorce was acquired limited the extent of a husband's power over a wife," she concludes.[17] Many unions were not viewed as binding contracts the way Euro-Canadian legal marriages were and, as a result, government Indian Agents forced Aboriginal couples to undergo (and pay for) legal marriages that restricted women according to patriarchal European and Christian customs. For example, in some First Nations, more than one woman might share a husband if the supply of men was insufficient. Regarding all such relations as polygamy, missionaries and Indian Agents argued that European-style marriage was in Aboriginal women's best interests. Conveniently, colonists and fur traders who had Métis or Indian country wives and were legally married to Euro-Canadian women living elsewhere were not viewed as polygamists.

Parliament enacted laws that gave Aboriginal husbands dominion over the assets of their wives. However, Aboriginal widows could obtain dower rights, or the right to a share of their husband's land and assets, "if a widow was determined by the Indian Agent to be living with him at the time of his death but only if she was of 'good moral character.'"[18]

Restricting the roles of Aboriginal women can be viewed as the lynchpin to securing white male dominance in their communities. First Nations societies unravelled as grandmothers lost their status as elders responsible for passing on traditions, knowledge and language. Starting in the late 1880s, Canada partnered with Catholic, Anglican, Presbyterian and United churches to establish boarding and residential schools for First Nations, Inuit and Métis children. Under the authority granted by the government of Canada, Aboriginal children were required by law to attend the residential schools. There, they were taught that their ancestors, culture and language were inferior to Euro-Christian beliefs and practices. Christianity was imposed and children were forbidden from speaking their languages, forced instead to speak English or French. Many children also suffered physical, emotional and sexual abuse at the hands of those responsible for their education and care.

Displaced by residential school teachings, women's role as teachers of customs and traditional practices was further undermined. Female status Indians were prohibited from voting in band elections and running for band office until 1951. Male and female status Indians only became eligible to vote in provincial elections in the late 1950s and eligible to vote federal elections in 1960.

COLONIAL WOMEN, 1630–1850

Women in religious orders were among the earliest administrators of seventeenth-century New France. As Candace Savage describes in *A Harvest Yet to Reap*, "For centuries, holy orders had been one of the few avenues open to women with ambition in community service or the professions."[1] Orders of nuns established hospitals, schools, orphanages and churches in New France and worked alongside the companies building the fur trade. While they did not set out to defy gender roles, their accomplishments stand in sharp contrast to the stereotype of nuns as religious handmaidens.

In 1639, Marie Guyart de L'Incarnation arrived to work as a missionary in the settlement that became Quebec City. Widowed at age nineteen, she left France and her eight-year-old son to head a group of Ursuline nuns who worked with the company operating the colony. Guyart is credited with building the first schools in Canada, and she oversaw the building of a convent. Guyart learned the Algonquin and Iroquois languages and composed dictionaries in Algonquin-French and French-Algonquin. Her influence in the colony was considerable, and governors consulted her on political matters.[2]

In 1642, Jeanne Mance arrived as part of a group that oversaw the settlement at Fort Ville-Marie, later Montreal. Mance was a member of the Society of Our Lady of Montreal, whose purpose was to convert the area's native inhabitants to Christianity and establish a colony. A founder of Montreal, Mance is credited with getting the settlement on strong financial footing. She opened Ville-Marie's first hospital, Hôtel-Dieu in 1645, secured funds from France to operate it and ran the hospital for seventeen years. Hôtel-Dieu followed the founding of a hospital in Quebec City by Marie-Madeleine de Vignerot, the Duchesse d'Aiguillon.

Marguerite Bourgeoys arrived in Ville-Marie in 1653. Her Congregation of Notre Dame of Montreal, an uncloistered religious community of nuns, worked directly in the community, rather than being restricted to working in convents. Bourgeoys oversaw the construction of buildings, including New France's first permanent church. She secured funding from the Catholic Church in France to operate a public school in 1658, to which both boys and girls were admitted. In 1676, Bourgeoys established a school, La Providence, for young girls. In 1982, she was canonized as Saint Marguerite Bourgeoys, Canada's first female saint.

While nuns helped create the settlement of New France, they could not populate the colony, in which men vastly outnumbered women. As such, Jean Talon, Intendant of New France from 1663 to 1673, arranged for several hundred young women, known as the *filles du roi* (the king's daughters), to be brought from France to grow the colony. Most of the women were married shortly after their arrival, at which time they were given a sum of money. Married settlers in New France received financial incentives to have children.

Married women in New France were under the rule of French law. According to Mona Holmund and Gail Youngberg, it was by decree of Louis XIV that "the law in New France was essentially the same as the Custom of Paris."[3] Under this group of civil or common laws, marriage created a community of property between a husband and wife. (English law, meanwhile, stipulated that a married woman's property belonged outright to her husband.) Under the Custom of Paris in New France, half of a couple's common property was inherited by the wife, the other half by their children (male and female). Widows in New France could inherit property their husbands had held under the seigneurial land distribution system, in place until 1854. This made it possible for some early colonial women to own property and establish businesses in New France.

Agathe de Saint-Père of Montreal was one such businesswoman. She bought and sold fur trade licences and land, and by 1705 she had developed unique textiles using fibres native to New France. When a textile shortage was worsened by the sinking of a supply ship en route to the colony, Saint-Père took matters into her own hands. First, she ransomed nine English weavers being held by Aboriginal allies of the French. She then built looms and secured apprentices, creating a successful textile manufacturing business.[4]

In 1757, colonial women in New France organized the first recorded women's protest in Canada. They took to the streets of Montreal to protest a decision of Governor Pierre de Rigaud de Vaudreuil to reduce public rations of bread and replace beef rations with horse meat while French and British forces were engaged in the Seven Years' War. In spite of Vaudreui's threats to hang the ringleaders, four hundred women marched in protest of reduced rations a year later and were successful.

At least two women who defended their interests during conflicts were later recognized for their efforts. Madeleine de Verchères, a fourteen-year-old Quebec girl, was one of them. In October 1692, the daughter of François Jarret, a seigneur in New France, and Marie Perrot, took up arms when Fort Verchères, on the shore of the St. Lawrence, came under attack during an Iroquois raid while her parents were away on business. Verchères is said to have climbed the fort bastion wearing a soldier's hat and fired the cannon to warn neighbouring forts and to call for reinforcements. Following her father's death, Madeleine received her father's pension in recognition of her role in directing the defence of the fort, with the stipulation she care for her mother.

Laura Secord made history during the War of 1812 while her husband, James Secord, was recovering from wounds he received during the Battle of Queenston Heights in Upper Canada. American forces occupied the Niagara Peninsula, including the town of Queenston, where the Secords lived, and American military personnel occupied their home. Secord overheard the military officials discussing details of a planned attack against British forces and, on a June morning, set out on foot to inform Lieutenant James FitzGibbon at DeCew House in a British-controlled territory some twenty miles away. Secord's tip is credited with the British victory at the Battle of Beaver Dams. However, her contribution went unacknowledged until 1860, when Edward, Prince of Wales, awarded her with £100 for her service.

Cross-dressing was another way for women to traverse gender and geographic boundaries. Of the estimated four hundred women who disguised themselves as men and fought in the American Civil War, at least one of them was a Canadian: Sarah Emma Edmonds, whose memoir, *Nurse and Spy in the Union Army*, was published in 1865. In order to avoid an arranged marriage at age fifteen, Edmonds left home and, after cutting her hair, took on the identity of Frank Thompson and found her way into the U.S. army. After training, Edmonds was assigned duty as a nurse and postman for her brigade.

Frank Thompson became an expert at disguise, eventually working as a Union army spy, and was disguised at times as a male or female slave. Upon her death in 1898, Edmonds was buried in the Washington military cemetery.[5]

Another woman who worked as a man was Margaret Bulkley, who hailed from Ireland. Documents indicate that Bulkley assumed a male identity, adopted the name James Miranda Barry and graduated from the University of Edinburgh medical school. In 1813, Dr. James Barry became a surgeon and joined Britain's army medical department. A visionary physician, Barry championed improved medical care in aid of lepers, slaves and the mentally ill. Barry served in Canada from 1857 to 1859 as Inspector General of military hospitals in Montreal, Quebec City, Toronto and Kingston. During her stint in Canada, Barry helped to improve sanitation, the diets of soldiers and the medical care of prisoners. Upon Barry's death in 1865, a charwoman who took care of the body revealed Barry's female anatomy.[6]

U.S. SLAVERY AND SUFFRAGE

By the middle of the 19th century, women involved with the U.S. anti-slavery movement began to push for greater civil rights for women as well as Black people. Many of these women were Quakers. The religious teachings of Quakers embraced a belief that women could minister for their faith, and many female Quakers were outspoken advocates for abolition and women's rights.

In the 1830s, Quaker sisters Sarah Grimké and Angelina Grimké inspired audiences with impassioned speeches denouncing slavery. They slowly won converts with their arguments in favour of rights for women. In *Letters on the Equality of Sexes and the Condition of Women*, published in 1838, Sarah Grimké wrote: "I ask no favours for my sex. All I ask of our brethren is that they will take their feet from our necks and permit us to stand upright on the ground which God has deigned us to occupy."[7]

Male abolitionist leaders generally didn't see a relationship between the subjugation of slaves and that of women. At a historic 1840 anti-slavery convention in Britain, female delegates were barred from the plenary floor and sequestered to a roped-off chamber to observe the proceedings.

Abolitionists Lucretia Mott and Elizabeth Cady Stanton, who had been in attendance at the 1840 conference, went on to organize the first North American gathering for women's rights in Seneca, New York, on July 19 and 20, 1848. The delegates, which included Black abolitionist leader Fred Douglass, passed resolutions calling for an end to all laws that placed women under the control of men. They issued a Declaration of Sentiments, which read in part:

> We hold these truths to be self-evident: that all men and women are created equal; that they are endowed by their Creator with certain inalienable rights; that among these are life, liberty and the pursuit of happiness; that to secure these rights governments are instituted, deriving their just powers from the consent of the governed. Whenever any form of government becomes destructive of these ends, it is the right of those who suffer from it to refuse allegiance to it, and to insist upon the institution of a new government, laying its foundation on such principles, and organizing its powers in such form, as to them shall seem most likely to affect their safety and happiness.[8]

Black women were unenfranchised on the basis of both race and gender. In 1851, Sojourner Truth, a former slave and a suffrage advocate, addressed a women's rights convention in Akron, Ohio, where a clergyman had expressed his view that women were too delicate to vote. Truth bowled over the crowd, challenging his race and gender assumptions:

> The man over there says women need to be helped into carriages and lifted over ditches, and to have the best place everywhere. Nobody helps me into carriages or over puddles, or gives me the best place — and ain't I a woman?[9]

The influential suffrage leader Susan B. Anthony visited Canada frequently and inspired Canadian women to take up the cause. In 1869, the National Woman Suffrage Association was formed in the U.S. and a few years later suffrage was on the women's agenda in Canada. While the U.S. made progress on women's rights more quickly than Canada at the end of the nineteenth century, Canada was a more hospitable jurisdiction for those fleeing slavery.

SLAVERY AND WOMEN

According to Joseph Mensah, author of *Black Canadians*, Jean Talon, during his tenure as Intendant of New France, which started in 1665, imported slaves from Africa. Wealthy merchants also brought slaves to New France, according to historian Constance Backhouse in *Colour Coded: A Legal History of Racism in Canada 1900–1950*. There are also records of Aboriginal people who were enslaved in New France. The arrival of slaves from Africa to New France, says Mensah, led to a decline in the proportion of Canada's Aboriginal slaves.[10]

It is estimated that there were some 4,200 enslaved people in the colonies, mostly confined to domestic service. One notable story from 1734 centres on an enslaved woman named Marie-Joseph

Angélique, who reportedly angry at the prospect of being sold, set fire to the home of her owner, Thérèse de Couagne. The fire spread, destroying forty homes as well as the Hôtel-Dieu de Montréal. Afua Cooper, author of *The Hanging of Angélique*, describes how Angélique was subjected to a form of torture that shattered the bones in her legs. After a confession was extracted, Angélique was executed by hanging. Within a Canadian context, Angélique's story is described as "the first recorded resistance to the cruelty of slavery by a black woman."[11] In 1763, following the British Conquest, General Jeffery Amherst confirmed that "all slaves would remain in the possession of their masters."[12] Then, following the American Revolutionary War in 1783, some three thousand Black loyalists were given passage to British North America by the British. Promised land as a reward for their service to the British, most Black Loyalists settled in Nova Scotia. But the land grants they were promised either did not materialize, or were smaller or of poorer quality than those given to white Loyalists. In response to the harsh conditions, which included racial antagonism, twelve hundred Nova Scotians left Canada in 1793 to help establish a colony for former slaves called Freetown in Sierra Leone.

Slavery was phased out in Canada starting in 1793, shortly after Chloe Cooley, an enslaved Black woman in Queenston, was forcibly bound and taken across the river to be sold in the U.S. Within months, "an Act to prevent the further introduction of slaves, and to limit the term of contract for servitude" was passed by the Upper Canada legislature. It stated that no additional slaves could be brought into the territories. It went on to state, however, that children born to "negro mothers" were to remain in the service of their mothers' owners until age twenty-five.

The first person to challenge slavery in what is now Canada was a New Brunswick resident named Nancy Morton. Born in Maryland

and brought to the colony in 1785 with her Loyalist owner Caleb Jones, Morton challenged the legality of slavery in a Fredericton, New Brunswick, court in an 1800 case, R *v.* Jones. Local lawyers Ward Chipman and Samuel Denny Street argued her case, and after the four-man court returned a split decision, Morton was forced to return to Jones. While ultimately unsuccessful, Morton's case helped turn public support against slavery.[13]

The British Parliament, in 1807, banned the importation of slaves into Britain and its colonies. However, the ownership of existing slaves and their children continued under domestic laws until August 1, 1834, when slavery was abolished throughout the British Empire, including Canada.[14] Slavery continued in the U.S., even though importing slaves had become illegal. Thousands of enslaved people fled for Canada after the passage of the notorious Fugitive Slave Act in 1850, a U.S. law that compelled authorities in northern states to return slaves (or suspected slaves) to their owners.

It was during this time that Harriet Tubman began helping slaves and free Blacks enter Canada West around Niagara Falls. According to historian Merna Forster, Tubman, who had been born on a Maryland plantation in 1820 to slave parents, transported some three hundred refugee slaves on the Underground Railway to Canada. According to Rosemary Sadlier, author of *Harriet Tubman: Freedom Seeker, Freedom Leader,* Tubman led nineteen freedom rides between 1850 and 1860. She earned the name Black Moses and was aided in her efforts by freed slaves and white abolitionist households. Tubman's reputation led the U.S. Society of Slaveholders to put a bounty on her life: $40,000 dead or alive.[15]

A brilliant strategist and adept at disguises, Tubman eluded U.S. bounty hunters. The gun-toting Tubman allowed no fires on her "freedom rides," in spite of the often cold weather. She also refused

Underground Railway conductor Harriet Tubman helped 300 former slaves to settle in Canada West.

to allow anyone to turn back, lest they be forced to reveal details of the Underground Railway.

Tubman settled in St. Catharines, where an estimated 123 Black settler families lived in 1855, including Tubman's elderly parents, who she brought to Canada West.[16] She was also an executive member of the Fugitive Aid Society, a benevolent society set up by former slaves to provide support to former "fugitive" slaves. Tubman returned to the U.S. when the American Civil War broke out, working as a nurse and a spy. She became the first woman in American military history to plan and conduct an armed expedition — the Combahee River Raid — which liberated more than seven hundred enslaved people in South Carolina. With her wages, Tubman financially supported schools for Black children and a home for the aged. She also found time to deliver speeches in support of female suffrage.

Another notable woman who moved to Canada after the passage of the Fugitive Slave Act was Mary Ann Shadd, born to free Blacks in 1823. Shadd's parents housed fugitive slaves on the Underground Railway. Shadd was educated for six years at a Quaker school in Pennsylvania and worked as a teacher before moving to Chatham, Ontario. In 1852, Shadd authored a booklet, *Notes of Canada West*, aimed at encouraging Blacks from the U.S. to settle in Canada West. Shadd opposed the creation of Black-only settlements and segregated schools, however, and this view that put her at odds with many Black settlers.

In particular, Shadd's views were oppositional to those of influential Black abolitionists Henry Bibb and Mary Bibb, publishers of Windsor's abolitionist newspaper *Voice of the Fugitive*. Mary Bibb is also credited with starting what is believed to have been the first women's literary society in Canada, the Windsor Ladies Club, in 1854. Such societies functioned as mutual aid societies and often served as platforms for political debate and civic action when necessary.[17] Bibb also taught Black children at a school she operated.

When Mary Ann Shadd started a newspaper, the *Provincial Freeman*, in the spring of 1853, she became the first solo Black female newspaper publisher in Canada. The *Provincial Freeman* discussed the problems of newly settled Blacks and the newspaper was anti-segregation in its outlook. Shadd also supported the involvement of women in public affairs and gave lectures in the U.S. to encour-

Mary Ann Shadd published the Provincial Freeman, *which discussed topics relating to Black settlement.*

age Black settlement in Canada West. In 1854, Shadd moved the newspaper to Toronto, where the Black population numbered more than a thousand. Her sister-in-law, Amelia Freeman Shadd, ran the *Provincial Freeman* when Mary Ann travelled, and helped fund it through the Ladies Literary Society of Chatham, which Amelia had founded. The *Provincial Freeman* reported favourably on a Toronto visit by well-known American suffragist Lucy Stone in 1855. Mary Ann Shadd wrote that "in Toronto, with the strong attachment to antiquated notions respecting women and her sphere so prevalent, [Stone] was listened to patiently and applauded abundantly."[18]

Shadd's views on Black settlement were not the only controversy she faced. When she first published the *Provincial Freeman*, Samuel

Ward, a Presbyterian minister, was listed as editor. By 1854, however, the masthead named "M.A. Shadd" as editor and readers likely assumed that the editor was a man. When Shadd's editorship was revealed, some readers were angry and Shadd agreed to name another male editor, Reverend William Newman. In 1855, the *Provincial Freeman* relocated to Chatham and it closed in 1857.

In 1856, Shadd married Thomas Cary and the couple had two children before Cary died in 1861. Following the end of the American Civil War, Shadd returned to the U.S. and went on to be the first Black woman to graduate from Howard University School of Law, at age sixty.

In 1870, the Fifteenth Amendment granted suffrage to former male slaves and free Black men in the U.S. As they were still unenfranchised, Black women and white women both worked in support of suffrage in the U.S. However, most organizations were segregated along race lines. In fact, southern white suffrage organizations at times excluded Black women from their membership. Undaunted, the National Association of Colored Women, formed in 1896, began publishing the *Woman's Era*, a newspaper that supported female suffrage and the advancement of Black women.

In Canada, Black women had leading roles in literary societies, whose aims were to promote literacy, education and civic involvement. Euro-Canadian women, in contrast, were often excluded from membership in literary societies run by Euro-Canadian men and were sometimes regarded with derision when they set up their own clubs: "Women's wish to socialize without men aroused deep-seated suspicion and their desire for self-improvement and even pleasure generated charges of selfishness."[19]

4

WOMEN AT CONFEDERATION, 1850–1899

While confederation aimed to give British colonies a measure of control over their governance, women in the new dominion still had few freedoms. Married women in particular faced unique forms of discrimination that restricted their property ownership and control of their wages.

PROPERTY AND MARRIAGE

Under British "coverture," enshrined in common law, a married woman did not have a separate legal existence from her husband. A married woman was a "feme covert" — a dependent, like an underage child — and her possessions were legally absorbed by her husband upon marriage.[1] In some Canadian jurisdictions, a property-owning woman was required upon marriage to obtain a new title replacing her name with her husband's. Women in Quebec were also legally subsumed by their husbands.

Inspired by the gains of the American sisters in New York State who successfully lobbied in 1849 for the right to hold property in their own names after marriage, women petitioned the legislature of Canada West for the right to keep property and possessions after marriage. In 1852, Anne Macdonald led a group of petitioners, Elizabeth L. Hawley and others petitioned the province in 1856, and another delegation followed the next year. The petitioners argued that a law was necessary to protect women whose drunken husbands gambled or drank away women's earnings and other assets.[2]

In 1859, a small gain came when Canada West enacted a law that stipulated that a married woman's property could no longer be sold by her husband without her consent. The law also set out a process whereby a married woman could obtain a protection order for her earnings, as well as those of her minor children, and could spend them without her husband's consent "in a variety of cases in which the husband was unfit or in which she was living apart from her husband for any reason which by law justifies her leaving him."[3]

After Britain relaxed its prohibition on married women owning property in 1872, a statute was enacted to give married women control of their wages. It would be twelve more years before Ontario's 1884 Married Women's Property Act granted women the right to own property and to enter into contracts involving property, including the right to sell property in their name without their husband's permission.

Property ownership conferred status in the rapid expansion of the West. Manitoba's 1871 Act Respecting Married Women stipulated that a woman kept her property upon marriage. However, it also stated that a married woman's earnings belonged to her husband unless he was cruel, insane, drunken or neglectful. A year later, when the 1872 Dominion Lands Act was enacted to encourage settlement on the prairies, single women were barred from obtaining a homestead. Homesteads were tracts of 160 acres of land for which males over eighteen years of age, on payment of a fee of $10, could apply. Only female heads of households with dependent children — widows

— could apply. The reasoning of Canadian officials was not that single women were incapable of homesteading. Rather, it was the position of the Department of the Interior that if single women could homestead, they might not bother to marry. Georgina Binnie-Clark, whose application for a homestead in Saskatchewan was refused because she was single and female, led a campaign against the discriminatory land act. Though her campaign was not successful, Binnie-Clark eventually purchased a farm and became a successful farmer and writer.

In most of English Canada, women fell under British dower law, which stipulated that widows had a one-third life interest in marital property if their husbands died. The concept of dower rights dates back to ancient Babylon and is mentioned in the Magna Carta. However, in western Canada, dower rights were abolished in 1886. "When the HBC [Hudson's Bay Company] monopoly collapsed great fortunes were to be made in the west and the new imperial and patriarchal goals for the region rested on complementary assumptions of British superiority and white male dominance."[4]

Divorce laws further restricted married women. Under the Matrimonial Causes Act of 1857, a husband had the power to divorce his wife if she committed adultery. However, a husband's adultery was insufficient for a woman seeking divorce. In order for a woman to obtain a divorce, her husband had to have been found guilty of adultery compounded with cruelty, or with desertion for two years, or incestuous adultery, rape, sodomy or bestiality.[5]

Bestiality evidence notwithstanding, the prohibitive cost of divorce made it virtually unattainable for all but the wealthy. A fee of $200 had to be paid before the divorce would be considered and the power to grant divorces resided with Canada's all-male parliament. According to Sarah Carter, author of *The Importance of Being Monogamous: Marriage and Nation Building in Western Canada to*

1915, the merits of a divorce case were debated "often by the prime minister himself."[6]

As a result, only about twenty divorces per year were granted in Canada between 1867 and 1913.[7] Meanwhile, it was declared in Quebec in 1866 that marriage for Roman Catholics was only dissolvable by death. As a result of these impediments, many people simply remained legally married while living in subsequent relationships.

WOMEN UNITE

The movement for women's emancipation began when women met under the auspices of discussing literary matters and civil topics. As they became more ardent in their quest for equal citizenship rights, they grew more confident in the names chosen for their organizations.

Emily Howard Stowe grew up in a Quaker household in Norwich, Ontario. In her family, education was considered as important for girls as for boys. In 1853, when she was fifteen years old, Stowe began working as a teacher, and later became the first female principal of a public school in Canada.[8]

After Stowe's husband contracted tuberculosis, she applied to medical school, but was refused admittance to the University of Toronto's Medical College on the basis of her sex. Stowe was accepted at the New York Medical College for Women, and her three children lived with her sister while she studied. In 1867, Stowe graduated and became the first female physician to practise medicine in Canada.

Stowe had a flourishing Toronto practice of mainly female patients on Church Street at a time when Ontario's medical college refused to grant medial licences to female physicians. Stowe and another female medical school graduate, Jennie Trout, were eventually allowed to attend a term of lectures at the University of Toronto in 1871 in preparation for their medical licences. Unfortunately, the women were subjected to fierce harassment by male medical students. In the end, Trout obtained her licence ahead of Stowe, who didn't receive a medical licence until 1880, when she was fifty. Stowe gained notoriety in 1879 after one of her patients, a pregnant and unmarried domestic worker, died. Stowe was charged with performing an abortion and, after a much-publicized trial, was acquitted. Stowe also helped establish the first women's college to train physicians in Canada.

Stowe became a leading proponent of women's rights. After attending a Cleveland, Ohio, meeting of the American Society for the Advancement of Women, she and a group of women established the Toronto Women's Literary Club in November 1876, the first women's organization in Canada to identify itself with suffrage.[9] Since female suffrage was not a popular cause, women's clubs often took on names that sounded politically benign. Besides, "literary" had been code for "politics" since the British bluestockings sought the education of girls. As well as female enfranchisement, the Toronto Women's Literary Club sought to improve conditions for women who worked in factories and championed the right of women to attend the University of Toronto.

Another founding member of the Toronto Literary Club was Sarah Anne Curzon. A writer, she became an associate editor of the *Canadian Citizen*, a temperance newspaper, where she wrote a regular column on women's rights. Curzon was author of *Laura*

This ad for Dr. Emily Stowe's medical practice appeared in the Toronto newspaper the Globe.

Secord: The Heroine of 1812, regarded as the first feminist play in Canada. The drama, which was published in 1887, was intended to set Secord in her proper place as a Canadian hero. In an 1890 interview with Montreal's *Dominion Illustrated*, Curzon said, "I trust that the time is not too far distant, when our men, laying aside their selfishness, jealousy and prejudice, may say to women, come over and help us, not only in making pure and righteous homes, but in making our nation."[10]

In 1883, the Toronto Women's Literary Club was reconstituted as the Canadian Women's Suffrage Association. It also permitted men as members. However, Stowe commented that the decision to admit men into the organization had been "demoralizing." Women members began to "rely on the gentlemen rather than upon their own efforts," she observed.[11]

Stowe was part of a delegation by the Women's Christian Temperance Union in 1889 that unsuccessfully petitioned the Ontario legislature to allow widows and spinsters to vote. In 1890, the organization, now called the Dominion Women's Enfranchisement Association, organized a national convention attended by a hundred women, including delegates from outside Ontario.[12]

Stowe's daughter, Augusta Stowe-Gullen, picked up her mother's political torch and became the first woman to complete medical training at a Canadian university when she graduated from Victoria University, Toronto, in 1883. Stowe-Gullen, a founder of the National Council of Women, was elected in 1892 to the Toronto School Board. Elected president of the Dominion Women's Enfranchisement Association in 1903, Stowe-Gullen believed that, "when women have a voice in national and international affairs, wars will cease forever."

TEMPERANCE AND SUFFRAGE

A critical influence on the suffrage movement in North America was the cause of temperance. Temperance adherents believed that alcoholism and the social ills that it spawned could be stopped by banning liquor sales. Many of them also believed that drunkenness should be grounds for divorce.

However, temperance and women's rights got off to a rocky start. After suffragist Susan B. Anthony was banned from speaking at a New York temperance meeting in 1852, she and other women started the Women's State Temperance Society. In 1853, the majority of its members scoffed at radical ideas like suffrage for women and divorce reform, preferring to focus strictly on the prohibition of alcohol.

Then, in 1874, the same year the Women's Christian Temperance Union (WCTU) was founded in Cleveland, Ohio, Canadian teacher Letitia Yeomans established a WCTU branch in Picton, Ontario. A popular public speaker in Canada, the U.S. and abroad, Yeomans became president of the Ontario and the Dominion WCTU. She started several branches, including those in Toronto and Montreal, and she set out to organize public votes, or plebiscites, to ban alcohol sales in municipalities. At the Dominion WCTU's 1888 convention, the national organization endorsed women's suffrage.

A philosophically Protestant organization, the WCTU came to support women's suffrage after plebiscites to ban liquor sales repeatedly went down in defeat. WCTU members came to believe that if women could vote, the plebiscites would pass. The WCTU resolution for female suffrage stated, in part, that "as God … has provided us with all the qualifications which make intelligent helpful voters, and added to them, that tender and vital interest in the human race which inheres in womanhood and maternity, we will never rest until we can fight Christ's battles armed with ballots."[13]

Temperance adherents blamed many modern social ills such as prostitution, violence, poverty, child neglect and family breakdown on alcohol consumption. Tales of violent, alcoholic husbands who squandered meagre family earnings on alcohol were widespread. The WCTU held that alcohol use was often at the root of violence against women and children, a situation worsened by the fact that women had no right to a share of their family's belongings if they became divorced.

The WCTU had more than a hundred branches in Canada. In rural and urban communities, members organized petitions and held public debates, not only on alcohol and the woman question, but also on prison reform, improved working conditions for female factory workers, child welfare laws, the reform of prostitutes and world peace. An 1893 Manitoba WCTU resolution stated, "we will never cease our efforts until women stand on an equality with men, and have a right to help in forming the laws which govern them both."[14]

WCTU members and other women's reformers worked side by side to circulate petitions and lobby for female enfranchisement. While they did not always agree on the root causes of the problems faced by women, their memberships nonetheless overlapped. Ultimately, their combined efforts improved the conditions in which women lived.

Due to women's efforts, laws were passed requiring husbands to provide financial support to their wives and children after separation. In Newfoundland in 1872, women could seek financial support from deserting husbands and, in 1880, Ontario followed. In Manitoba, a woman with a drunken or irresponsible husband could ask for a court order freeing her from the obligation to live with him. Women in Saskatchewan and B.C. won the right to apply to the courts for custody of their children and seek financial support upon divorce.

THE GROWTH OF WOMEN'S CLUBS

Increasingly, women were taking an active role in public affairs through women's clubs, which provided a forum for debate on social and legal reforms and also provided direct services and programs aimed at helping women and children. An expanding era of volunteerism brought women together to establish libraries, teach hygiene and improve prison conditions.

The first branch of the Young Women's Christian Association (YWCA) was founded in 1870 in Saint John, New Brunswick. It concerned itself with the welfare of single women newly arrived in Canada and provided them with temporary lodging, recreation and Bible study. The national YWCA was formed in 1895.[15] The Ladies' Hebrew Benevolent Society of Montreal, created in 1877, helped Jewish families who arrived from Europe. More than a dozen Jewish women's organizations started during this time to provide support to Jewish families in difficult circumstances, including the Daughters of Israel in Saint John, New Brunswick, in 1899. The National Council of Jewish Women of Canada was formed in 1897. The Colored Women's Club of Montreal formed in 1902.

Inspired by the formation of the International Council of Women in 1888, the National Council of Women of Canada was formed in 1893 to unite associations of women working for the betterment "of conditions pertaining to the family and the state."[16] Its aims included social reform and its members would work on issues of common ground to Protestant and Catholic groups, Jewish groups, self-help groups, urban groups and rural groups. The Council's first president, Ishbel Aberdeen, was also president of the International Council of Women. Aberdeen's husband, John Campbell Gordon, known as the Earl of Aberdeen, was governor general of Canada between 1893 and 1898. The National Council immersed itself in social and legal issues affecting women. Due to the fact that the National Council was an umbrella organization, its survival depended on its members' ability to focus on common causes.

One of the first issues discussed by the Council was the need to improve low wages and poor working conditions for female factory workers, who earned as little as $2 per week.[17] The Council conducted research on factory conditions and shops acts across Canada so that Council women could circulate petitions and exert pressure on governments. Local councils pushed for mandatory school attendance as a means to undermine child labour, and members were encouraged to lobby provinces to hire female factory inspectors.

Although often categorized as a somewhat conservative organization, the National Council of Women did manage to ruffle feathers. Facing down strong opposition from male doctors, Aberdeen, who was also known as Lady Aberdeen, and Council members started the Victorian Order of Nurses (VON) in 1898 to provide nursing

Members of the National Council of Women of Canada, founded in 1893.
Credit: Library and Archives Canada, PA-028035.

and midwifery services in remote areas where physicians were rare.[18] VON training homes were established in Ottawa, Montreal, Toronto and Halifax. Matters of public health were among the uppermost concerns of the National Council of Women at a time when standards tended to be haphazard. Typhoid outbreaks led the group to petition for water filtration, and the organization first proposed a national department of health in 1905.

Meanwhile, Catholic Church officials in Quebec forbade Catholic women's groups from associating with the Council when its resolutions veered too strongly in favour of rights for women, as it did in 1910 when the National Council of Women finally supported women's suffrage.

Women's Institutes were a vital support for rural women, starting in 1897 in Stoney Creek, Ontario.[19] Women's Institutes carved out a strong domestic niche driven by the efforts of Adelaide Hoodless of Hamilton, Ontario. After Hoodless's infant son died from drinking contaminated cow's milk (a common cause of infant death, referred to as the "summer complaint"), she made it her life's work to educate girls and women on nutrition and sanitation in the home. Hoodless, who did not advocate suffrage, oversaw the development of programs dedicated to "domestic sciences." Women's Institutes lobbied successfully for the pasteurization of milk. Hoodless later convinced tobacco company owner William Macdonald to fund a private college to teach domestic science. The Macdonald Institute went on to develop programs for institutional dieticians and later, for teachers of domestic science in schools.

Within ten short years, there were five Women's Institutes in Canada. Beginning as a support network for rural women, the Women's Institutes aimed to develop informed citizens and to work for national programs to achieve common goals. Women's Institutes later moved into the classroom where they initiated the instruction of domestic science, as well as music classes: "There is no doubt that the present welfare provisions in Canada are built upon, and take much of their character from, the achievements of this type of volunteer activity."[20]

THE EARLY WOMEN'S VOTE

In 1841, the first national assembly was elected in the province of Canada, which was made up of Upper Canada and Lower Canada. Interestingly, there was nothing in the 1791 Constitutional Act to specifically bar women from voting, although voting requirements made it all but impossible for most women to vote. Would-be voters had to own property or have assets of a specified value, or else pay a minimum rate of taxes or rent. Voting was done orally and openly; both corruption and violence were rampant.

In Lower Canada (Quebec), women were not subject to English common law, but rather the custom of Paris, which allowed women to acquire half of the marital property when their husbands died. As a result, some propertied women in Lower Canada voted between 1809 and 1849. Manon Tremblay, the author of *Quebec Women and Legislative Representation* recounts an 1809 account of the widowed grandmother of Louis-Joseph Papineau casting her oral vote for her son, "Mr. Joseph Papineau, as I believe that he is a good and faithful subject."[21]

It is likely that some propertied women in the Maritimes also voted in the early 1800s because women were singled out to be disenfranchised by laws introduced in Prince Edward Island in 1836, in New Brunswick in 1843 and in Nova Scotia in 1851. Then in 1849, the Reform government (a precursor to the Liberal Party) of the province of Canada enacted a law to standardize voters' lists in Upper and Lower Canada. At that time, women were banned from voting: "May it be proclaimed and decreed that no woman shall have the right to vote at any election, be it for a county or riding, or for any of the aforesaid towns and cities," the law stated.[22]

Notwithstanding this prohibition, property-owning women obtained the municipal vote in many jurisdictions. A suffrage bill was introduced in the B.C. legislature in 1872 and property-owning female British subjects[23] in B.C. were the first to be granted the municipal vote in 1873.[24] In 1882, the municipal franchise was granted to property-owning widows and spinsters in Ontario.[25] Suffrage supporter Liberal John Waters, a member of the Ontario legislature, introduced suffrage proposals every year starting in 1885. Non-married propertied women in New Brunswick gained municipal voting rights in 1886. By the next year, propertied women in Nova Scotia and Manitoba had a municipal vote, and in 1888 Prince Edward Island women were similarly enfranchised. In Montreal, "widows and single women, whether home owners or renters, had been entitled to vote at [the municipal] level since 1887."[26] Propertied women commonly voted in school board elections.

After the imposition of the Indian Act in 1876, Ontario decreed that in places where no electoral lists existed, Aboriginal men who renounced their Indian status could vote provincially if they were not "residing among the Indians" or receiving annuities from the Crown. Others who received annuities from the Crown, including tax collectors and judges, were prohibited from voting. B.C. removed its property requirement for voting in 1876, but prohibited people of Asian descent, as well as Indians from voting.

In 1883, Prime Minister John A. Macdonald introduced a series of bills aimed at making voters' lists uniform. One of the proposals under his Electoral Franchise Bill would have granted single and widowed propertied women, as well as propertied Indians, the right to cast a ballot. MacDonald abandoned the measure, however. "The opposition to female franchise was centred in Quebec, but the proposal was lost when members from other parts of the country advised that they intended to vote against the proposition out of consideration for the feelings of their French-speaking colleagues."[27]

Suffrage petitions from the Canadian Women's Suffrage Association and the Woman's Christian Temperance Union were presented to Parliament in 1894 and 1896. Conservative MP Nicholas Flood Davin (Assiniboia West) introduced a resolution in 1895 in support women's suffrage. "Women are quicker in their perceptions than men," Flood Davin told Parliament during the debate. "To include them among the electorate would quicken the intelligence and perceptiveness of the constituency." The bill was defeated by a vote of 105 to 47.

At this time, a popular movement arose to end the property and income requirements. Casting a ballot came to be viewed as a right of citizenship, rather than a privilege for certain classes. Once the right to determine voting lists was confirmed under MacDonald's Electoral Reform Act to be a provincial matter, women's suffrage efforts turned closer to home. In 1894, following a national meeting at which the National Council of Women dissociated itself from the franchise movement, Manitoba's Equal Franchise Club was formed by journalist E. Cora Hind and Dr. Amelia Yeomans, a pioneering Winnipeg physician. Petitions for women's suffrage were presented by WCTU members to legislatures in Victoria and Winnipeg in 1894. A petition bearing two thousand names accompanied the bill introduced in the Manitoba legislature.[28] Suffrage petitions were also presented in Ontario, Quebec and Nova Scotia. In 1895, the Halifax WCTU organized a petition for suffrage that garnered twelve thousand names.[29] The outspoken Edith Jessie Archibald was WCTU Halifax's president and then occupied the position of president of the Halifax Victorian Order of Nurses from 1896 to 1906.

Nova Scotia's suffrage effort had the support of author Anna Leonowens, who had been a founder of the Halifax Council of Women in 1894. Leonowens had supported her two children by working as a governess to the wives and children of the king of Siam for seven years. Before moving to Canada in 1876, Leonowens wrote the 1870 book *The English Governess at the Siamese Court* and *The Romance of the Harem* (1872). Leonowens believed that as long as women were refused the right to vote, they should refuse to pay taxes. She was a founder of the Nova Scotia College of Art and Design in 1887.

After the Hudson's Bay Company relinquished its charter of Rupert's Land, the government of Canada entered into a series of numbered treaties with First Nations. The Crown then pursued a policy of rapid settlement expansion of the Prairies. A flood of Britons as well as immigrants from Russia, Ukraine, Iceland, Finland and Germany arrived, along with an influx from Ontario and the U.S. Soon, movements in support of temperance, women, farmers and workers coalesced under the umbrella of prairie populism. Farm women and WCTU members joined forces with female physicians and journalists who used their professional standing to advance the cause of women.

In Winnipeg, Dr. Amelia Yeomans was president of the Manitoba branch of the Dominion Women's Enfranchisement Association and president of the Manitoba WCTU from 1896 to 1897. She specialized in midwifery and diseases of women and children and practised medicine with her physician daughter, Lillian Yeomans, licensed in Manitoba in 1882. In addition to being a popular speaker on female suffrage and temperance, Amelia Yeomans advocated for non-English-speaking immigrants and the poor. She made connections between overcrowded housing and disease, and called for improved conditions for women in prisons and in factories. Yeomans also lectured on the spread of venereal disease, having witnessed its impact on prostitutes she regularly treated in her practice.

Although attempts to gain female suffrage in Canada in the late nineteenth century were not successful, women in New Zealand were enfranchised nationally on an equal basis with men in 1893, and South Australian women won the vote in 1895.

THE FIRST WOMEN'S STRIKES

Some 80,000 children were brought to work in Canada as farm hands and domestic servants between 1869 and 1924. Most were Irish, English and Scottish. As well, young single women from Britain and European countries were recruited to work in domestic service, wooed by advertisements sponsored by railway companies. The campaigns promised adventure, fresh air, decent pay, hard work and future husbands.[30] By 1891, there were 83,508 domestic servants and waitresses in Canada, according to the Dominion Bureau of Statistics. This represented 41 percent of the more than 203,000 girls and women in the official workforce.[31]

In some cases, employers advanced money for the voyage of a domestic worker to Canada. The domestic worker was required to pay back the sum and was under contract to work in their employer's home for twelve or fourteen hours a day with Thursday and Sunday afternoons off. A general servant in eastern Canada earned between $8 and $14 per month in 1900.[32]

Most women left domestic work in favour of factory work, the needle trades or employment in a shop, hotel or restaurant. Even work in an under-regulated, non-unionized factory was considered by young women to be more desirable than domestic work. The isolation and lack of privacy experienced by domestic servants were major complaints, and employers regularly held back their wages. Sexual exploitation was common, and while employment outside domestic work did not necessarily pay more or involve easier work, workers were not called upon twenty-four hours a day.

Although middle-class, Euro-Canadian women did not typically work outside the home after marriage, immigrant women and working-class women, as well as Black women and divorced or widowed women, commonly did. Young women could expect to work by age fifteen and their earnings were one-half to two-thirds of what men would be paid for similar work. As a result, women changed jobs frequently in search of better pay. Working-class women commonly worked as tailors or dressmakers, seamstresses, launderers or milliners for six and a half days per week.

The garment trade was highly segregated. Female sewing machine operators were considered unskilled, while the higher paid position of cutter was reserved for men, who were considered artisans. Female sewing factory workers earned about 83 cents per day, while male sewing factory workers averaged $1.46 per day. An 1899 newspaper article in *Citizen and Country* reported that workers who sewed Eaton's clothing in Toronto were

> locked out till noon if they are not at work fifteen minutes before eight o'clock in the morning — not a minute's grace is allowed although they all work by the piece. When they are in they are locked in, and are not allowed to leave the room, no matter what the cause may be, unless they procure a pass, written by one man and signed by another... If they

> break more than three needles per week they are charged
> for them at a much dearer rate than in other stores ... If an
> operator stands up from her machine before the bell tolls
> the hour of retiring, instant dismissal follows.[33]

Women and children often worked in dirty, poorly lit factories and textile mills where shabby toilets, a lack of heat and dangerous work were common complaints. In the Quebec cotton industry, almost half of the workers were women. In 1871, women and children made up 42 percent of the industrial workforce in Montreal and 34 percent in Toronto.[34] Twelve percent of Canadian girls and women were officially in the paid workforce.[35] Factory, textile and needle trades workers typically worked twelve-hour days with poor pay and few breaks. Poor ventilation meant that textile workers breathed in fibres that increased their risk of lung disease.

The right to strike was implicitly recognized by Canada's 1872 Trade Union Act, but employers still routinely fired union members. And while tradesmen belonged to a craft guild tradition that allowed them to bargain for wages and control the number of tradesmen in their profession, tradesmen did little to support women's early organizing efforts. Many male union members claimed that women's employment drove down the wages of men.

Few female workers were unionized; however, that didn't stop them from walking off the job. In 1880, Hochelaga, Quebec, weavers, led by female workers, struck to protest an imposed increase in their work week. The *Montreal Gazette* reported that while some men were among the strikers, the male workers "were not nearly so demonstrative as the women."[36]

In 1882, the first major strike of female workers in Toronto took place when 250 shoe and boot makers struck for improved pay and working conditions. The Knights of Labor supported women's strike actions and set up day nurseries for their children. The striking women from five factories sang a song about their grievances:

> We won't sew on a button,
> Nor make a button hole;
> We won't stitch up a shoe top,
> All ready for the sole,
> Until the price is raised a peg,
> On all the shops' pay roles.[37]

The female workers formed a committee to negotiate with the factory owners. Nine days after the walkout, male shoe and boot makers joined them in a sympathy strike. After three weeks, the employers promised to introduce a new bill of wages, and two-thirds of the workers voted in favour of going back to work. Unfortunately, the factory owners didn't keep their promise and, after the women struck again, a bill of wages for the shoe and boot makers was implemented in 1884, according to University of Western Ontario historian Greg Kealey.[38]

The Knights of Labor was more than a union organization. It was a progressive movement that advocated for cooperatives, supported high taxation for land speculators, favoured free and compulsory education and supported the nationalization of the railway. The Knights of Labor believed in organizing workers regardless of skill level or sex. Among those supported were male and female mill operatives in Ontario and Quebec. With the support of the Knights of Labor, women formed the Excelsior Local Assembly 3179 in Hamilton in April 1884. Assembly 3179, made up of shoe operatives, was the first all-woman local in Canada.[39] It was formed under Katie McVicar, a Knights of Labor leader. The Knights organized several women's locals in Ontario in the 1880s. The Knights of Labor's view differed from the craft union approach, which tended to view women as unskilled, temporary workers.

For some trade unionists, the answer to low female wages was to fight for higher wages for men; that way, women could return to their "rightful" place in the home. Many unions rallied behind the demand for a "family wage," a privilege to be reserved for male workers. Canada's Trades and Labor Congress voted in 1889 to prohibit girls and women from working in branches of industrial life including mines, workshops and factories. The Socialist Labor Party backed equal pay for equal work, but wanted girls and women banned from all jobs that could harm their health or safety.

Female factory workers sought greater economic benefits and improved work conditions. And yet, when Ontario and Quebec introduced factory acts in 1884 and 1885 to improve women's working conditions, the measures were often cited as proof that female workers were more vulnerable than male workers and therefore not entitled to equal benefits.

The Royal Commission on the Relations of Capital and Labour in 1887 confirmed that women were subjected to harsh treatment at work, including physical abuse. The commission recommended hiring female factory inspectors to enforce safety measures. However, the commission seemed at times more concerned with the corruption of women's morals than their labour rights, according to Ruth A. Frager and Carmela Patrias in *Discounted Labour: Women Workers in Canada, 1870–1939.*

As such, calls for "protectionist measures" for women were controversial. Some women opposed measures designed to ease women's working lives, believing they reinforced the idea women were incapable. And yet it is difficult to imagine arguing that an 1890 statute that forbade employers from "seducing" employees who were under twenty-one and "of previously chaste character" was not, in some ways, a positive step to fight sexual harassment. Similarly, it seems hard to view a law requiring shop owners to provide stools for the relief of saleswomen during ten-hour shifts as somehow coddling workers. Ontario was the first province to pass a law stipulating that young women could not be hired for factory work before age fourteen. The hours that women, girls and youths could work were also limited to ten per day, or sixty per week.[40] However, fines for violations were low and employers were rarely charged.

In 1891, over seven thousand girls under age sixteen were employed in the Canadian industrial sector. The Ontario Bureau of Industries calculated the annual average earnings of female workers without dependents as $216.71, while their annual costs were determined to be $214.28.[41] Complaints about unfair wages for women were frequently reported in Winnipeg's left-leaning newspaper, the *Voice*. In 1895, a delegation from the Manitoba Equal Suffrage Club addressed the Winnipeg Trades and Labour Council (TLC) to argue for equal pay for men and women in the same occupations. Dr. Amelia Yeomans advised the audience that the low wages paid to women undercut men's efforts to raise their own pay. If women could vote, she argued, they would have greater influence to better their work conditions. In 1898, following a presentation by E. Cora Hind, an influential *Free Press* agricultural writer and women's rights advocate, the Winnipeg TLC added women's suffrage to its agenda. The Canadian TLC also endorsed women's suffrage.

Meanwhile, a single woman fortunate enough to obtain a teachers' certificate could expect to earn $287 per year, just over half the salary paid to a male teacher. Under the conditions of her contract, a female teacher could be expected to agree not to frequent ice cream parlours, keep company with men, dye her hair, wear bright-coloured clothing or drive in automobiles with men who were not her father or brother. A female teacher would not live alone but would board with a family in the community. Her contract would not be renewed if she married.[42]

THE FIGHT TO ATTEND UNIVERSITY

In 1874, the first nursing school in Canada opened at the General and Marine Hospital in St. Catharines, Ontario. It was started by two nurses affiliated with British nursing pioneer Florence Nightingale. The first public health nurses visited the homes of the poor to educate mothers about infant health, diet and domestic sanitation.

In 1875, Grace Annie Lockhart became the first woman to receive a university degree at Mount Allison University in New Brunswick, making it the first university in the British Empire to award a bachelor's degree to a woman. At this time, most Canadian universities refused to grant women advanced degrees. It was not only administrators but students who wanted to keep women out. When Queen's University medical school agreed in 1881 to admit female students, male medical students revolted. They demanded that female students be expelled on the basis that anatomy topics were not taught in sufficient depth in the presence of female students. While their claim was not substantiated, the university capitulated. It set up separate classes for female medical students and refused to admit additional female students.

In response, a group of female medical school graduates from Queen's University opened Kingston's Women's College in 1883. Toronto's Women's Medical College opened the same year, with the support of Emily Howard Stowe. Starting in 1884, women were allowed to study medicine at the University of Toronto.

Then, in 1890, Maude Abbott received the Lord Stanley Gold

Medal at McGill University after graduating with her bachelor of arts, but was refused entry into medical school because she was a woman. Undeterred, she obtained medical training at Montreal's Bishop's University, received top prizes in her final year, and went on to study pathology in Vienna. Abbott became a world-renowned expert in congenital heart defects, wrote textbooks and published over a hundred research papers on the subject. In 1898, Abbott was appointed assistant curator of the McGill Medical Museum, but was refused a full professorship. In 1910, McGill still refused to grant medical degrees to women, but it awarded Abbott an honorary one. The University eventually appointed Abbott to its medical staff as a lecturer in pathology. When McGill graduated its first female medical students in 1922, the top student was a woman.

Clara Brett Martin fought a similar battle to open doors. She applied to the Law Society of Upper Canada in 1891, but was refused because of her sex. The law society refused to call women to the bar because the word "person" in the society's eligibility requirements did not, it determined, include women. Martin lobbied the premier and, with the support of the Dominion Women's Enfranchisement Association, won the right to study law in 1892. Martin graduated in 1895, and, after further wrangling, the law society admitted women in 1897. Law schools in Quebec kept their doors closed to women until 1941.

Canada's earliest female scientist, Harriet Brooks, enrolled at McGill University in 1894. A nuclear scientist, Brooks made the discovery that not only are elements transformed during radioactive change, but the product of that change is also radioactive and, in turn, becomes transformed.[43] Brooks worked in Paris with Marie Curie, who received the Nobel Prize for physics in 1903. When she married at thirty-one, Brooks retired from science. She died twenty-five years later from a blood disorder, believed to have been brought on by unprotected exposure to radiation.

Carrie Derick, a botanist who graduated from McGill University in 1892, became the first woman instructor appointed to the academic staff of a Canadian university. Derick was a pioneer in the study of genetics and heredity. In 1912 she became the first woman appointed as a full professor in Canada as a professor of comparative morphology at McGill University. "The professions should be open to men and women alike. It is just a question of the survival of the fittest," said Derick, who was also president of the Montreal Suffrage Association in 1913 and a popular speaker on women's rights and social reform.[44]

WOMEN OF THE KLONDIKE

The Klondike Gold Rush offered many women the promise of adventure, independence and good pay. In many ways, the confines of rigid sex roles were suspended in the early Klondike, where women staked claims for gold, ran hotels, worked in dance halls and operated laundries. Women opened restaurants and bakeries, provided massage treatments and worked as prostitutes in Dawson, the first city in western Canada to boast electric lights.

The textbook tale of the August 16, 1896, discovery of gold by George Carmack, a Californian, and two Tagish men seldom mentions the woman who played a central role in the discovery that led to the Gold Rush. Katie Carmack (Shaaw Tláa) was George Carmack's wife. She was a skilled hunter and cook who knew the difficult Chilkoot Trail area and, according to some accounts, George's first telling of the discovery credited Katie as the person who first discovered gold at Bonanza Creek. Nevertheless, the three men laid claims to the discovery. George became rich and left Katie in 1900 to marry a woman he met in Dawson. Katie Carmack never received her share of the family windfall, despite her legal attempts to do so.

Many women made their mark as Klondike entrepreneurs. According to Frances Backhouse, author of *Women of the Klondike*, Belinda Mulroney built the Grand Forks Hotel and owned a supply outlet. In 1898 she purchased a share in the Eldorado-Bonanza Quartz and Placer Mining Company and hired miners and a foreman to run her mining operation. "I only hired a foreman because it looks better to have it said that a man is running the mine," Mulroney said, "but the truth is that I look after the management myself."[45]

Martha Purdy made the gruelling trek up the Chilkoot Pass to Dawson City in the early stages of pregnancy and gave birth to a son in a cabin during the winter of 1899. Purdy later bought a saw mill and eventually married George Black, who became a member of Parliament. After George Black's death, Martha Purdy Black succeeded him, becoming Canada's second female member of Parliament in 1930, at age sixty-nine.

Brothels operated openly in the early days of the Klondike on some of the most valuable properties in town. Dancehall girls in Dawson earned good wages, between $8 and $12 a night; they earned commission on the drinks sold to patrons between sets. Meanwhile, the WCTU and the Salvation Army lobbied Ottawa to crack down. In 1902, an ordinance forced brothels to move from the town's centre.[46] While local saloon and hotel owners were not strenuously opposed to prostitution, many opposed the fact that brothels served alcohol and therefore competed with them for customers. One solution was the imposition of liquor licences that permitted only hotels, saloons and dancehalls to sell liquor. Another measure saw a fine of $50 imposed on prostitutes, with fees used to help pay for hospitals. A third measure saw doctors examine prostitutes every two weeks and issue a health certificate if they were free of venereal disease. The boom in prostitution ended when the Klondike gold supply dried up and thrill seekers moved on.

EARLY PRESSWOMEN

By the late1800s, reform-minded women in Europe and North America had begun publishing newspapers to increase support for women's rights. Luise Dittmar, a German writer, created the journal, *Soziale Reform*. In the U.S., Amelia Bloomer published the *Lily* in 1849 and Elizabeth Cady Stanton started the *Revolution* in 1868.

In Quebec, Josephine Marchand-Dandurand was editor of one of first women's publications in Canada, the French-language *Le Coin du feu* from 1893 to 1896. *Le Coin du feu*'s purpose, according to its publisher, was, in part, "to raise the intellectual level of the female sex."[47] Marchand-Dandurand was also an executive member of the National Council of Women of Canada and was an early proponent of government funding for the arts. Robertine Barry, an influential newspaper writer and social reform advocate, contributed to *Le Coin de feu*. In 1902, Barry started *Le Journal de Françoise*, a bi-monthly dedicated primarily to publishing the writing of women. Françoise was Barry's pen name.

Suffrage support was strong in Gimli, Manitoba, on the west side of Lake Winnipeg, an area settled by Icelandic settlers in the early 1870s. Icelandic immigrant Margret Benedictsson, who from 1898 to 1910 published one the first suffrage newspapers in Canada, *Freyja* (a Norse goddess of love, fertility, battle and death), championed improvements in the legal and social conditions of women and published articles on the need for divorce reform and state-sponsored welfare. It also supported temperance. *Freyja*, a forty-page monthly newspaper focused on "matters pertaining to the progress and rights of women," was published for twelve years with the help of Benedictsson's husband, Sigfus, with whom Margret operated a printing business. Benedictsson also founded the Icelandic Equal Suffrage Club in 1908 and was a popular public speaker on women's rights. An ardent believer that marriage should be a union of equals and that divorce must be easy to obtain, Benedictsson divorced her husband in 1910 and moved to the U.S. with their three children in 1912.[48]

The *Champion*, published by the B.C. Political Equality League, carried articles about legal rights for women and the problems of prostitution, suffrage and temperance. One of its regular contributors was WCTU member and Political Equality League founder Florence Hussey Hall. In one article, she wrote that the "women's movement has been called into existence to teach the world the value of human life and human freedom."[49]

Freyja, one the first suffrage newspapers in Canada, was published in Manitoba by Margret Benedictsson from 1898 to 1910.

Meanwhile, daily newspapers began to hire women in an effort to attract more readers. In 1886, Sara Jeannette Duncan became one of the first newspaperwomen hired to work full-time at a Canadian daily newspaper, Toronto's *Globe*. During her five years on the job, Duncan attended women's conventions and wrote about social issues, including suffrage, before moving to India, where she became a novelist. Kate Simpson Hayes was another early female presswoman in Canada. Following her move from New Brunswick to Regina with her two children, she started contributing to the *Regina Leader*, founded by Nicholas Flood Davin. Davin was Hayes' "long-time companion and the father of her two younger children," according to Susan Jackel, writing in *First Days, Fighting Days*.[50] In 1895, Davin, a conservative MP, introduced a bill in support of female suffrage in the House of Commons. Hayes, who published fiction under the pen name Mary Markwell, moved to Winnipeg and, in 1899, became the first women's page editor of the *Manitoba Free Press*.

Alice Freeman, a journalist and champion for women's rights, published under the name Faith Fenton. In 1894, at age thirty-eight, she quit her job as a school teacher to focus on writing and was hired as editor of the *Canadian Home Journal*. Fenton then accompanied stampeders to the Yukon to report on the Klondike Gold Rush in 1898. There, she reported on women who made the journey to Dawson on foot.

Kathleen (Kit) Coleman was a pioneering newspaperwoman who earned a wide following with her column "Kit's Kingdom," published in Toronto's *Mail and Empire* from 1889 to 1911. Born in Ireland, Coleman came to Canada as a widowed mother, remarried shortly after her arrival and turned to writing to support herself after the death of her second husband. Although not a proponent of female suffrage, Coleman advocated for prison reform, divorce reform and the right of women to enter all occupations. She also wrote on the need for race tolerance and supported environmental conservation. Coleman became Canada's first female war correspondent after she reported from Cuba at the end of the Spanish-American War in 1898.

Despite the tenacity of women reformers and some early successes in legal and education rights at the turn of the century, it would take the efforts of a new generation before many important gains, including female suffrage, were won.

THE SUFFRAGE ERA,
1900–1919

The first decades of the twentieth century marked the era of the "new woman." The Victorian period ended and women's hemlines and hair became shorter. It was a time when cities grew, electric street cars aided transportation, and people flocked to newly built theatres to watch live performances.

One of the most popular performers in the early 1900s was Pauline Johnson, a writer and poet who was also known as Tekahionwake (her Mohawk great-grandfather's name). Born near Brantford, Ontario, on the Six Nations Iroquois Reserve in 1861, Johnson's father was a hereditary Mohawk chief and her mother was British.

Johnson sometimes wore a buckskin dress during the first half of her performance to represent her native ancestry, while her costume for the second half was a European-style dress. Johnson confounded class and race stereotypes, and her work often addressed colonial issues from the point of view of Aboriginal people. Her poem "A Cry from an Indian Wife" was based on the Battle of Cut Knife Creek during the Riel Rebellion. The narrator speaks from the point of view of a woman whose husband is going to fight:

Go forth, and win the glories of the war
Go forth, nor bend to greed of white man's hands,
By right, by birth we Indians own these lands,
Though starved, crushed, plundered, lies our nation low...
Perhaps the white man's God has willed it so.

Her performances were widely acclaimed. Another popular poem was "The Song My Paddle Sings," a passionate ode to nature that reflected a woman's intimate relationship with her canoe and the rushing river. Johnson's writing was widely published, starting with a book of poetry, *White Wampum,* in 1895. Her final book of stories was published in 1913, following her death.

"Pauline Johnson's life and work suggest an implicit effort to reconcile and integrate insights of Natives and New Women in a critique

Pauline Johnson performed on stage both in buckskin dress and in European-style clothing.

of the dominant race and gender politics of her day," according to Veronica Strong-Boag and Carole Gerson, authors *of Paddling Her Own Canoe: The Times and Texts of E. Pauline Johnson Tekahionwake.* "The new woman," the authors wrote, "signalled modernity in her espousal of many causes, including better education, paid work, egalitarian marriage, and health and dress reform to improve her own lot and that of her sex in general."[1]

The number of women

reformers who earned their livelihoods as writers continued to grow during the suffrage era. According to Carol Bacchi, author of *Liberation Deferred? The Ideas of the English Canadian Suffragists 1877–1918*, a quarter of suffrage leaders in English Canada were published writers. There were more than a hundred women writing for newspapers and magazines.

To unite them, the Canadian Women's Press Club was started in 1904 as a professional association and a hub of political reform activity. The club came about after *Halifax Herald* staff writer Margaret "Miggsy" Graham lobbied CPR publicist George Ham for access to free railway passes being given to journalists covering the 1904 World's Fair in St. Louis.[2] Graham, at the *Halifax Herald* since 1898, saw to it that sixteen presswomen, half of whom were from Quebec, travelled free to the fair. Upon their return, the presswomen decided to form a professional association, as women were barred from joining the all-male Canadian Press Club.

Kit Coleman of Toronto became the club's first president in 1906 at the first national meeting of the Canadian Women's Press Club, which drew forty-six delegates to Winnipeg. Succeeding Coleman was Montreal's Robertine Barry. The post was then held by Kate Simpson Hayes, women's editor at the *Manitoba Free Press*. Another Canadian Women's Press Club member of note was the "man-suited" E. Cora Hind,[3] who had been agriculture editor of the *Manitoba Free Press* since 1902. Hind was exceptionally skilled at predicting the size and quality of wheat harvests, and her predictions helped determine the price of prairie wheat for twenty-five years. A newspaperwoman for forty-one years, Hind was active in the early WCTU and was a founder of the Manitoba Equal Suffrage Club.

Flora McDonald Denison was a dressmaker turned presswoman. Her columns, published in Toronto's *Sunday World* from 1909 to

1913, championed the need to improve the conditions of women in the needle trades. McDonald Denison became president of the Dominion Women's Enfranchisement Association in 1911.

Popular prairie presswomen included sisters Francis Beynon and Lillian Beynon Thomas. Beynon Thomas worked as an assistant editor and women's columnist at the *Manitoba Free Press* starting in 1907. She published stories about abandoned wives and destitute widows who needed laws to establish their right to family property following death or divorce. Beynon Thomas was an organizer of Women's Institutes. After Beynon Thomas and her husband Vernon Thomas were fired from the *Manitoba Free Press* as a result of their anti-conscription views during the First World War, the couple moved to New York.

Francis Beynon took up journalism six years after her older sister. She was hired as editor of the women's pages of the *Grain Growers Guide* in 1912 after working in advertising at the T. Eaton Company. Farm women on the prairies were galvanized by letters and articles published under Beynon's watch. They were angry they were not entitled to an automatic inheritance of the family farm if their husbands died, even though they worked the land equally hard. And they were desperate for information on birth control. Beynon helped mobilize women to take up political causes, including the right to homestead and to vote.

Beynon wrote in a 1913 editorial: "We have too long been contented with the kind of motherhood that can look out of the window and see little children toiling incredible hours in factories and canning sheds over the way… and say calmly, 'Thank God, it isn't *my* children.'"[4] And yet neither Beynon, who was single and had no children, nor other women who embraced the suffragist label, believed that women should resign themselves to being strictly mothers and housewives. As Beynon wrote in one editorial: "As nearly as I can find out, it was by no divine revelation that this conclusion was reached. Some man said so and it was echoed around the world because most men felt so. They decided that woman's place was the home, because they wanted her to stay there. I never yet knew a man who had any fondness for washing dishes and scrubbing floors, so they think it is the ideal work for a woman."[5]

WOMEN AT WORK

In 1901, 14.4 percent of girls and women over age fourteen were in the paid workforce. They made up 14.9 percent of the labour force. Employment for the estimated 240,000 female workers included domestic work, the needle trades, retail sales, the manufacturing sector, cotton mills, teaching, laundry work, hotels, restaurants, factories and fisheries. Domestic workers made up 30 percent of women in the workforce, a proportion that would decline to 20 percent after the First World War.[6]

In the Quebec cotton industry, almost half of the workers were women, while a quarter of those working in manufacturing were women. By 1911, the number of women in the paid workforce rose to 365,000. Census figures did not include the estimated 7,500 women in Toronto and 9,000 women in Quebec who did piecework for the garment industries in their homes. Children often helped by removing basting threads from the garments or by sewing on buttons. Nor did official tallies include the Maritime women who boxed factory-made candy in their homes.[7]

Official figures also did not count women who farmed with their husbands, although about half of Canada's population lived in rural areas. In the cities, white-collar work opened up to women, providing employment in stores and in offices such as telephone companies. Many managers believed female workers were better than male workers at handling impolite customers. A few women were employed as stenographers and "type writers." However, employing women to type was still considered a radical experiment in the early 1900s.

The Toronto Dominion Labour Council in 1902 supported women's demands for equal pay, equal civil rights and for the abolition of labour for children under age fifteen. Although very few women were unionized, that didn't stop women from striking for improved wages and conditions. In 1907, four hundred telephone operators struck against Bell Telephones of Ontario when the company offered a meagre wage increase while increasing workers' hours by 50 percent. Telephone operators' work was constant and stressful, and few breaks were given. Workers frequently experienced shocks and were closely monitored by supervisors. They wore six-pound headsets while they worked. Those who joined the electrical workers union during the strike were told to resign from the union or lose their jobs. Deputy Minister of Labour William Lyon Mackenzie King persuaded the operators to go back to work in exchange for a public inquiry; their hours of work were eventually reduced.

According to Mildred Gutkin and Harry Gutkin, authors of *Profiles in Dissent*, "a vigorous recruiting drive brought union organization to all but one of Winnipeg's garment factories by 1905." There were frequent firings by clothing manufacturers of union members following work stoppages and picket lines were increasingly defended by equally aggressive male and female workers.

It was during this era, in 1910, that International Women's Day was born at the Second International Conference of Working Women, held in Copenhagen. German socialist Clara Zetkin tabled the motion and delegates from seventeen countries endorsed the establishment of International Women's Day to demand improvements to women's working lives. It was first marked on March 19, 1911, with public protests for suffrage and improved work conditions, but would later be marked on March 8th.

The vulnerability of female factory workers was underscored on March 25, 1911, when 146 workers at the Triangle Shirtwaist Company in New York died in a blaze, during which the building's exits were locked. Of the dead, 129 were Jewish and Italian female immigrants. Many jumped to their deaths, engulfed in billowy flames, as they fell ten storeys. The tragedy helped challenge the stereotype that female workers were temporary participants in the labour force who didn't deserve the same benefits and protections enjoyed by male workers.

In Canada, the 1911 B.C. Factory Act restricted women's work to eight hours per day within a forty-eight-hour work week. In response to women's lobby efforts, provinces began to hire female factory inspectors.

In 1912, about a thousand Eaton's workers in Toronto, many of them Jewish employees, walked off the job. The strike started when sixty-five male cloak makers, members of the International Ladies Garment Workers' Union, refused to take on extra piecework that was normally performed by female finishers, for no additional remuneration. When the company fired the male protesters, the largely female workforce walked off the job. The female employees, who were non-unionized, had their own list of grievances, including poor wages, a thirteen-hour work day and sexual harassment. The strike spread to Eaton's in Montreal, and a Jewish-led boycott of Eaton's goods was organized. Workers returned to work after four months with little success to show for their efforts, and Eaton's continued to stymie organizing efforts.

Six hundred telephone operators in Winnipeg joined a union in 1917 and successfully struck for a salary increase from $35 a month to $40 a month and a forty-hour work week.

Women's labour leagues (WLL) started during this time. They were not chiefly made up of unionized women, but rather tended to be composed of wives of unionized labourers. The leagues often supported women's organizing efforts and helped women whose husbands were on strike. "Some were wage-earning women; and many were Finnish-, Yiddish- or Ukrainian-speaking," writes Joan Sangster in the *Canadian Encyclopedia*. "The WLL platform, radical for its time, included demands for equal pay, maternity care and birth control."[8]

Nursing continued to be a low-status, low-paying occupation when Ethel Johns graduated from the Winnipeg General Hospital Training School for Nurses in 1902. There were only three hundred trained nurses in Canada at the time, and, according to Johns, "young students were exploited by the hospitals as a source of cheap labour."[9] Johns was instrumental to the professionalization of nursing in Canada and established the Department of Nursing at the University of British Columbia. She also worked internationally to expand public health nurse training.

In 1903, the first meeting of the University Women's Club was held in Toronto. At a time when women were still barred from many university faculties, university women's clubs pushed for greater educational opportunities for women and an end to discrimination in the workplace. Local branches across Canada advocated for social, legal and economic reforms including equal pay and suffrage. They also lobbied governments to improve factory conditions, establish minimum hours of work per day for women workers and eliminate child labour.

Racial discrimination in employment and education was still widespread. Mary Matilda (Tilly) Winslow McAlpine was the first Black woman to attend the University of New Brunswick, and she graduated in 1905 with a bachelor of arts degree. Unable to find work in Canada, McAlpine moved to the U.S. and became dean of the Education Department at Central College in Alabama.[10]

Increasing industrialization and rapid immigration changed the economic and social landscape during this time. In the first two decades of the twentieth century, more than half a million people from the British Isles and a quarter million people from the U.S. arrived in Canada. Another half million immigrants from Europe and Asia came to Canada. While Canada welcomed many immigrants, Chinese immigrants were singled out to pay a head tax of $500 in 1904. As a result, Chinese men could not afford to bring their wives. Some young women from China were brought to Canada under the guise of being daughters of Chinese merchants, when in fact they were impoverished Chinese women forced to work as domestic servants or in restaurants.[11]

WOMEN IN QUEBEC

Marie Gérin-Lajoie joined the Montreal Council of Women in 1900, but found the group too Anglophone for her interests. So, in 1907, she founded the Fédération nationale Saint-Jean-Baptiste (FNSJB) with an aim to reform laws in support of women, who had no legal standing over family matters. Two other co-founders were Joséphine Marchand-Dandurand and Caroline Béique, who served as its first president.[12]

Quebec feminists faced fierce opposition from Catholic clergy, who claimed that the Church and not the state should be the arbiter of moral issues. Both conservative and liberal politicians, backed by clergymen, claimed that women's emancipation posed a threat to the French Canadian family and, by extension, to Quebec society itself. Women's suffrage was positioned by opponents as an English concept, and therefore as a threat to Quebec society.

Undaunted, the Fédération nationale Saint-Jean-Baptiste set up thirty branches in the following decade.[13] The Fédération also organized classes to train domestic workers and provided women with pure milk for their children. One of the Fédération's accomplishments was the 1908 creation of the province's first institution for higher education of Francophone women, École normale supérieure de jeunnes filles. Gérin-Lajoie was the author of two books on the legal status of women: *Traité de droit usuel*, published in 1902, and *La femme et le code civil*, published in 1929. Both books articulated the need for improved legal rights for married women in particular, and later, some of the reforms were adopted in Quebec's Civil Code.

Quebec women did not win the provincial franchise during this time. They were, however, successful in establishing a juvenile court in 1920, a children's aid society and a reform schools for wayward girls. In Quebec, as elsewhere, it was young women from lower classes who were sent to such schools in an effort to divert them from going to jail following arrests linked to prostitution, unwed pregnancy and public drunkenness. The new institutions gradually replaced Catholic-run institutions.

Many working women in Quebec saw improvements. The authors of *Canadian Women: A History* wrote: "By 1914, Quebec women teachers' pensions had doubled, factory lighting had improved, pure milk depots or 'Gouttes de lait' had been established to reduce rampant infant mortality, and legislation was passed making it mandatory to provide female store clerks with chairs."[14]

HOW THE VOTE WAS WON

The Dominion Elections Act made it clear that the only people who could vote in a federal election were those eligible to vote in a provincial election. Efforts to secure female suffrage, therefore, went exclusively provincial. After women the New Brunswick Political Equality League

Newfoundland suffragists succeeded in obtaining the female franchise in 1925.
Courtesy of Gertrude Crosbie and the Archives and Manuscripts Division Collection 158, Queen Elizabeth II Library, Memorial University, St. John's, NL.

started in 1902 to lobby for suffrage, women in B.C created the Political Equality League of Victoria in 1908, followed by a Vancouver Political Equality League. In 1911, they jointly formed a B.C. Political Equality League, led by long-time temperance leader Maria Grant. In Toronto, the Canadian Suffrage Association and the Ontario WCTU held a large public demonstration in 1909 at the Ontario legislature.

The fight for female suffrage also gained momentum on the Prairies, which was becoming a hotbed of social radicalism that had its roots in labour, farm, social gospel and women's movements. Support for female suffrage could be found in labour newspapers like the *Winnipeg Voice*, although the workers' paper took exception with suffragists' focus on sex oppression over class oppression.

Nellie McClung, a best-selling author and former WCTU activist, moved to Winnipeg in 1911 from Manitou, Manitoba. The city was already bustling with political activism. McClung and writer Lillian Beynon Thomas lived in the same neighbourhood. Beynon Thomas was elected president of the Manitoba Political Equality League when it was founded in 1912 at the home of Jane Hample on Wolseley Avenue. The League's founders determined that it couldn't be left up to the local Council of Women to lead the fight for the vote, as many considered suffrage too radical. "Their husbands wouldn't let them 'go active,'" McClung mused in her autobiography, *The Stream Runs Fast*. "We believed that 15 good women who were not afraid to challenge public opinion could lay the foundations better than a thousand. Some good work had already been done by the Icelandic women of the city, who had organized the first suffrage society many years before, and the WCTU women could always be counted on and the same was true of labor women."

Women's organizations frequently worked together. McClung and a representative of the Council of Women, Mrs. Claude Nash, persuaded Manitoba Premier Roblin to tour a Winnipeg sewing factory following the 1911 Triangle Shirtwaist Factory fire in New York. Women at the Winnipeg factory worked for nine and a half hours per day. The factory had no fresh air in the summer and no heat in winter, and the premier reportedly called it a "hell hole." Roblin was asked to hire a female factory inspector, but he refused.

Nellie McClung joined the suffrage community in Winnipeg when she arrived from Manitou, Manitoba, in 1911.

In 1911, the B.C. Women's Suffrage League was started by British-born Helena Gutteridge, a trade union activist, tailor and pacifist. Gutteridge was the first woman to sit on the province's Trades and Labor Council. She also worked to establish mother's pensions (welfare) and later became Vancouver's first alderwoman in 1937, representing the Co-operative Commonwealth Federation.

Anglophone women in Montreal, led by Carrie Derick, a geneticist and the first female professor in Canada, founded the Montreal Suffrage Association in 1913. In a *Montreal Herald* article November 23, 1913, Derick wrote: "The spirit that animates the movement is not self-seeking. It is rather, a maternal spirit aroused by infant mortality, the exploitation of child labour, the evils of prostitution, the hardships of the sweated worker and the greater property placed upon property than upon the persons of women."

The term "maternal feminism" is widely used by modern observers to classify feminists who argued that, as mothers and wives, women brought special qualities into the political sphere. However, it is worth considering whether women like Derrick were simply being strategic in employing terms such as "maternal spirit." After all, women were regularly denigrated as selfish and unnatural when they demanded equal legal rights. Repeatedly, from the political right and the political left, by church patriarchs and pressmen alike, women were told that only matters involving children and their home should concern them. Likewise, most politicians steadfastly refused to support women's suffrage on the basis that it would destroy families.

Given this opposition, it would not have been surprising if women had strategically called their opponents' bluff and turned their maternal gunfire against them. It also bears mentioning that many early suffragists who invoked such arguments, including Derick, were not married and did not have children.

Sly mockery of their opponents was, in fact, a popular tactic of suffragists. In one of the highlights of Manitoba's fight for the vote, a mock parliament was held in 1914 to raise funds for the suffrage battle. Harriet Walker, a member of the Political Equality League, was the Walker Theatre's co-owner. Before a packed house of supporters, women assumed the roles of politicians in a burlesque role reversal. The all-women legislature heard a delegation of men plead for the vote. "Premier" Nellie McClung brought down the house with laughter when she mocked Premier Rodumund Roblin's words and told the audience: "Politics unsettles men, and unsettled men means unsettled bills, broken furniture, broken vows and divorce. The modesty of our men, which we revere, forbids us from giving them the vote. Man's place is on the farm."

A vital force in the suffrage movement in Manitoba, McClung

moved to Alberta with her husband and five children in 1915. After Roblin was unseated, the province's new Liberal premier, T.C. Norris, asked women to again demonstrate that Manitobans supported woman's suffrage. This time, nearly forty thousand signatures were presented on petitions to the legislature, including a second petition that included 4,250 names amassed single-handedly by ninety-year-old Amelia Burritt.

On January 28, 1916, Manitoba became the first province to extend the franchise to women on equal terms with men. Some savvy last-minute lobbying by Frances Beynon and Lillian Beynon Thomas ensured the bill was amended to include the right of women to be elected to the legislature as well. McClung astutely captured the scope as well as the limitations of the vote when she said, "The government has enfranchised you. But it cannot emancipate you. That is done by your own process of thought."

Saskatchewan followed in March 1916 and Albertan women were next to get the provincial franchise in April 1916. In Edmonton, McClung, Emily Murphy and Alice Jamieson celebrated by buying new hats and having a group photo taken. In February 1917, Ontario women were enfranchised, followed by British Columbia women in April 1917. Nova Scotia women were enfranchised and had the right to sit in the legislature in 1918, while women in New Brunswick could vote in 1919, though they did not have the right to be elected to their legislature until 1934. Prince Edward Island ended its male-only franchise in 1922, while Newfoundland women were allowed vote only in 1925. Women in Quebec did not obtain the provincial vote or the legal right to run for political office until 1940.

The toehold gained by women reformers in matters once considered the private domain of the family and the church forever changed Canada in the early years of the twentieth century. Women's efforts helped carve out an expanded role for the state in the area of social policy and public health. The vote was simply a tool they sought to increase women's voice in public affairs.

In Saskatchewan in 1911, Violet McNaughton advocated state-supported medical care, including public hospitals. Her campaign called for "medical aid within the reach of all."[15] In 1913, McNaughton helped found the Women Grain Growers in Saskatchewan and was president of the organization for its first three years. Two decades before the CCF took up the cause, McNaughton led the Women Grain Growers' (WGG) crusade for government funding to train midwives, nurses and doctors and for municipalities to provide grants to hospitals. In 1916, Saskatchewan founded union hospitals and hired municipal nurses and municipal doctors. In 1916 Annie Gale of Calgary formed the Women Rate Payers Association, which lobbied for municipally funded hospitals. She later became the first female city councillor when she was elected in Calgary.

McNaughton was a proponent of grain marketing to stem the exploitation of western farmers and also helped draft the platform of the Progressive Party, which would later be folded into the Co-operative Commonwealth Federation. She became an influential member of the Saskatchewan Wheat Pool, which evolved into the largest producer cooperative and grain handler in Canada. "The efforts of Violet McNaughton and the WGG led to the development of a health care system, which was an important step in the eventual creation of Medicare in Canada," notes Merna Forster, author of *100 Canadian Heroines: A Celebration of Herstory.*

FIRST WORLD WAR

At the start of the First World War in 1915, women made up 15 percent of the workforce, a proportion that hadn't changed significantly in nearly twenty years.[16] However, the number of women in the workforce increased as a war-related shortage of young male workers grew, and by the end of the war, women made up 25 percent of the workforce in some parts of the country. Work in non-traditional fields of industry, such as boilermakers and welders and in the munitions industry, expanded women's skills.

Women were instrumental to Canada's war effort, but they were also resented. While war industry profits rose, wages remained lean and some tradesmen opposed the presence of women in traditionally male occupations.

Thirty-five thousand women worked in munitions factories in Ontario and Quebec, and the work conditions were often difficult. A group of female munitions workers appealed to the *Toronto Star* in 1917. "They are killing us off as fast as they are killing the men in the trenches," declared the group's spokeswoman, explaining that the women worked six days a week, all but one for twelve hours.[17] The war also saw a trend towards hiring women to fill jobs as bank tellers (previously considered a male job) as well as other white-collar jobs.

During the First World War, there were 3,141 nurses in the Canadian Army Medical Corps. Women worked overseas in armed forces camps in bakeries and kitchens, as clerks, typists, telephone operators, dieticians and nurse's aides. As more soldiers were killed and more men behind the scenes moved in to take their places on the front lines, women took on more jobs as drivers and mechanics.[18]

Nurses treated wounds, attended surgeries and bore witness to the horrors of war. They wrote letters to soldiers' families and sometimes worked eighteen-hour days. Many worked near the front lines. According to the Canadian War Museum, there were fifty deaths from enemy fire, disease or drowning among the 2,504 nurses who served. On June 27, 1918, a German U-boat torpedoed and sank the Canadian hospital ship *Llandovery Castle*, killing all fourteen nurses on board.

Canadian women's organizations back home raised money to finance ambulance services staffed by women's brigades known as Voluntary Aid Detachments (VAD). VAD members drove ambulances, picked up wounded soldiers and transported the dead. They worked twelve-hour shifts, with half a day off per week. According to Debbie Marshall, author of *Give Your Other Vote to the Sister*, the VAD provided many women with a "socially acceptable opportunity to shake the dust from their heels." Marshall notes: "Some were galvanized by the same things men were — a hunger for adventure, a desire to serve the Empire, and the opportunities to gain social status through military service."

Some fifteen thousand women in Newfoundland supported Canada's war effort by joining the Women's Patriotic Association effort to knit socks, scarves and mittens, and sew clothing and bandages for soldiers. Ontario Women's Institutes sent $1.65 million in goods to soldiers overseas.

A number of women opposed Canada's involvement in the war. Canadian members of the Women's International League for Peace and Freedom, founded in 1915 by 1,300 women from Europe and North America, were also active in farm, labour and women's organizations. One of them was Ontario's Agnes Macphail, who would become the first woman elected to the House of Commons and later help found the Co-operative Commonwealth Federation. One of the founders of the Women's International League for Peace and Freedom, Jane Addams, received the Nobel Peace Prize in 1931.

A handful of female journalists went overseas to file reports about the war for Canadian newspapers. Mary MacLeod Moore with *Saturday Night*, Elizabeth Montizambert of the *Montreal Gazette*,

Florence MacPhedran of the *Toronto Daily Star* and Beatrice Nasmyth of Vancouver's *Daily Mail* filed articles from France. Considered too fragile to be exposed to the horrors of war, female reporters were assigned to write emotional tales about the brave women behind the scenes. With wartime propaganda constraints in place, stories were designed to provide a lift for those back home whose sons were facing possible conscription.

THE BATTLE OVER CONSCRIPTION

"It seems like a horrible nightmare that we are picking out our big, stalwart young men and instructing them hour after hour, in the ways of death," wrote pacifist and Manitoba newspaperwoman Frances Beynon.

Prime Minister Robert Borden faced a dilemma heading in to the 1917 federal election. Thousands of soldiers had already lost their lives, and Borden was determined to step up Canada's war effort with mandatory military service. He knew he could count on enlisted servicemen for support, but he needed more pro-conscription votes, and Quebec, non-British immigrants and unionists were against conscription.

Borden soon came up with a scheme to divide his opponents and win re-election. His manoeuvrings not only split the opposition Liberal Party (many Liberals joined Borden's Union government), but he also pitted women's suffrage interests against their patriotism and invoked closure to his plan to increase the number of voters who would support him. The conscription debate was bitter on many fronts.

The battle lines were drawn in 1917 when Borden suddenly expressed support for the female franchise after a trip to Britain, reversing his early position. Borden said that because of their war efforts, women "had made clear their right to a voice in the government of their country."[19]

However, the prime minister's stance on suffrage turned out to be a Trojan horse. He intended to give only select women a vote. First, his Military Voters Act would give all Canada's military personnel overseas, male and female, the vote, including those under the legal voting age of twenty-one. The property requirement for voting was also removed. Next, the Wartime Elections Act extended the vote to wives, widows, mothers, sisters and daughters of those, alive or deceased, male or female, who had served overseas. The Wartime Elections Act also disenfranchised many immigrants who had been born in "enemy alien" countries (unless they had already enlisted or had a relative who was enlisted). Most of those disenfranchised were born in Germany or Austria-Hungary, and four thousand of those who were deemed a risk were interned in camps in Canada during the war.

Women's organizations, including local councils of women, rejected the idea of limiting the franchise to women with relatives at war. Women should receive the vote based on their status as equal citizens, they believed, and not as pawns in Borden's war effort. The president of the Canadian Suffrage Association remarked at the time that Borden's bill would have been more honest if it had simply disenfranchised everyone who failed to promise to vote for Borden's Union government. Other women supported Borden. In Saint John, N.B., the president and vice-president of the Women's Enfranchisement Association resigned in 1917 after the organization's members refused to endorse Borden's Union government.

When the war first broke out, Nellie McClung was an ardent pacifist. She wrote: "The fall of 1914 blurs in my memory like a troubled dream. The war dominated everything ... British peers held stocks in the Drupp Works in Germany … One of the first guns captured from the Germans … was found to have been made in England … War was a game, a plot against humanity and would go on for as long as the common people could be depended on to do the fighting."[20] McClung's sentiments shifted, however, when her oldest son enlisted at age eighteen. She hoped that an Allied victory would see her son return alive. "What have I done to you, in letting you go into this inferno of war?" she wrote after her son's departure in 1915, "And how could I hold you back without breaking your heart?" McClung, forty-two at the time, observed that she lost her youth when her son went to war. Watching the war divide friendships also took its toll. She reflected how, during the war, "the old crowd began to break up and our good times were over."

In 1916, the year before Borden's measures were implemented, McClung expressed support for the idea of a partial franchise for women as a war measure. She changed her mind, however, after listening to the views of suffragists like Francis Beynon, the women's page editor of the *Grain Growers' Guide*. Borden's proposal, Beynon said, would have excluded some foreign-born women from voting. In a letter published in the *Guide*, McClung withdrew her partial franchise support. She went on to say that a united effort by women "cannot be jeopardized by a difference of opinion over a method of procedure." She further added, "I know one person's judgment is liable to be faulty."[21] McClung did not support Borden's disenfranchisement bill. Busy working in support of American women seeking the franchise at the time of Canada's first federal election in which some women were enfranchised in 1917, McClung did not cast a ballot.

Borden's war measures passed and he won re-election. Prime Minister Borden then hosted a women's war conference in Ottawa in

February 1918. It marked the first time the federal cabinet had officially consulted with women from across Canada. More than seventy prominent women representing women's organizations attended the conference. Attendees called for minimum wage laws for women, equal pay, universal women's suffrage and free technical training for women. The Alberta delegation insisted that Canadian grain being shipped overseas be milled beforehand to ensure it was used for food, not liquor. The National Council of Women of Canada repeated its call for the creation of a federal department of health. Its members had declared at its 1917 convention that "it is the duty of the State to provide care and training for those who are either permanently or temporarily unfit for normal life."[22]

Following the war, Borden's disenfranchisement measure was rescinded and a federal bill was introduced in May 1918 to grant suffrage to women aged twenty-one and over. In the wake of the Borden conscription scheme, however, federal suffrage was a bittersweet victory.

As a result of women's extensive achievements during the war, their claims of entitlement to the rights of citizenship gained greater legitimacy, including the right to equal pay and the right to hold political office.

THE FIRST ELECTED WOMEN

While the spotlight on the women's social reform movement dimmed after the vote was won, its leaders went back to work. They returned to matters of improved work conditions, legal reforms and lobbying for better public health services and child welfare policy development.

In 1917, WCTU organizer and social reformer Louise McKinney was elected to the Alberta legislature, the first woman in Canada elected to represent a provincial riding. Because Alberta created two additional seats to represent the interests of those serving in the war, a second woman, Roberta McAdam, an enlisted dietician serving overseas, was elected by enlisted personnel in the same election as McKinney.

McKinney advocated for improved working conditions for miners and for better laws to protect immigrants. Her main issues were divorce reform and property rights to help women, who were frequently rendered penniless upon the death of a husband or upon divorce. She also helped in the formation of the United Farmers of Alberta.

Emily Murphy was the force behind Alberta's dower law — a provision to reinstate the right of wives a minimum one-third interest in their husbands' estates upon their death. Murphy gave public speeches on women's rights and in support of a children's protection act, a law that would establish in law that children could obtain protection from neglect and abuse.

Appalled at the treatment of poor and marginalized women by the justice system, Murphy successfully lobbied the Alberta government to establish a separate women's court. She was then appointed a magistrate in 1916, the first woman in Canada to hold the position. McClung, a Liberal, was elected to the legislature in 1921, along with Irene Parlby, who represented the United Farmers of Alberta. Edmonton suffragist Alice Jamieson was also a magistrate in the juvenile court.

Helen Gregory MacGill was a central figure in the women's movement in B.C. A member of the University Women's Club of Vancouver, she lobbied B.C. to make its inheritance and custody laws fairer to women. Although not a lawyer, MacGill was appointed as the first female juvenile court judge in B.C. in 1917. MacGill was an early proponent of the idea that juvenile delinquency was linked to social factors, including poverty. She advocated for a social welfare system to reduce crime and lobbied for female police officers and female probation officers.

In 1918, Mary Ellen Smith of B.C. became the first female cabinet minister in Canada. Like McKinney, McClung and Parlby in Alberta, her aim in seeking office was to improve the lives of the disadvantaged. A Liberal, Smith was responsible for legislation that included the Juvenile Courts Act, the Deserted Wives Maintenance Act, the Equal Guardianship Act, the Nurses' Act, the Act Regulating Night Employment for Women and the Mothers' Pensions Act.[23]

LABOUR WOMEN RISE UP

Following the war, jobs for returning soldiers were scarce and anti-immigrant sentiments increased. Labour unrest was widespread throughout Canada, and workers were angry that manufacturers who profited from the war refused demands for better pay and a forty-hour work week. Wages plummeted and inflation made women's already low wages even less adequate. At the same time, many people demanded that women should be shut out of "men's jobs." Unionized iron moulders in Ontario struck to prevent women from being hired, according to Ruth A. Frager and Carmela Patrias in *Discounted Labour: Women Workers in Canada, 1870–1939*. Toronto streetcar operators threatened to strike if women were hired.

Women continued to defend their right to work. "And now the war is over and people are anxiously asking, 'Will women go back?' Is it reasonable?" queried Nellie McClung. "After you have used an electric washer, will you go back to the washboard or the two flat stones in the running stream?"[24]

The University Women's Club went to work. It had determined that a single, self-supporting woman required a bare minimum of $10 per week. However, women who worked in department stores were regularly paid just $9 per week. Women were unapologetic about their need to work and strikes showcased women's growing labour militancy. Helen Armstrong, president of the Hotel and Household Workers' Union in Winnipeg, had been a tailor by trade. She was a boisterous force on picket lines from 1917–1920 and her husband, George Armstrong, was a commanding public speaker on the principles of Marxism. The Armstrongs and other socialists had opposed conscription during the war under the slogan "No conscription of manpower without conscription of capital."

As president of the Women's Labour League, Armstrong organized soup kitchens for striking workers and the league provided support to the wives of strikers. Armstrong helped organize Winnipeg's five-and-dime-store workers into the Retail Clerks' Union in 1917. After one unsuccessful strike by the union, a report on women workers was commissioned by the Board of Labor to determine a minimum wage for women. According to Mildred Gutkin and Henry Gutkin, authors of *Profiles in Dissent: The Shaping of Political Radicalism in the Canadian West,* the Manufacturers' Association included an annual clothing budget for factory girls in its submission, prompting Armstrong to comment: "No furs provided for thirty below, merely a scarf, and this advocated by men who appear in beaver coats, otter caps and warm overshoes."[25]

In Ontario, the Women's Social-Democratic League was formed to advance the aims of socialist women. Labour women in Manitoba successfully campaigned for Manitoba's Minimum Wage Act, passed in 1918. It set up a board to set minimum pay rates for women who worked in shops and factories. Manitoba's law stipulated that two of the five board members were to be women — one representing labour and other management. Next, trade unionist Helen Gutteridge organized the campaign that led to B.C.'s minimum wage law for women. Quebec and Saskatchewan followed in 1919, while Nova Scotia and Ontario passed minimum wage laws in 1920. Alberta amended its Factories Act to protect female workers in 1920.

Improved wages were a top priority for women, though few were unionized. While women made up only 13 percent of the 24,000 strikers during the 1919 Winnipeg General Strike, they played a leading role in the strike from day one. At seven o'clock on May 15, 1919, five hundred "Hello Girls" unplugged their switchboards and abandoned their posts, four hours ahead of the 11:00 a.m. time that the Strike Committee called for a work stoppage.[26] The telephone operators were the first to walk out. Seven hundred female bread and cake workers walked out early too, shutting down all but one of the city's confectionery plants. Retail clerks, garment workers and waitresses also voted in favour of the strike. The Women's Labor League provided 1,500 meals per day for strikers in soup kitchens. About a dozen women were arrested during the strike, mostly for intimidating strike breakers.

The Winnipeg General Strike was crushed after the federal government called in the militia, deported foreign-born workers and threw strike leaders in jail. Thousands of male and female workers were fired, yet the strike intensified the spirit for labour reform, not only in Manitoba, but also in British Columbia, Alberta and Ontario, where smaller general strikes were held. In Manitoba, strike organizers were elected to the legislature and to the House of Commons. A dozen years later, reformers from across Canada would form a political party, the Co-operative Commonwealth Federation, to advance the political interests of labour and farmers to support a wide range of reforms being put forward by women.

6

THE INTER-WAR YEARS, 1920–1939

Women's lives changed dramatically during the inter-war years. Infant mortality improved and women were having fewer children. In 1920, there were 102 infant deaths per thousand births in Canada, a drop from 184 infant deaths per thousand births in 1851. Most births still took place at home, although there would be a shift to hospitals by 1940. The average age of marriage for Canadian women in 1921 was 24.3 years.

By the time the inter-war period was over, most homes in large urban settings had running water and electricity; cleaning clothes no longer occupied two full days of work. Improved sanitation also meant a reduced burden on women to care for sick family members.

The Prohibition many women supported came into effect as part of an effort to preserve grain resources, under the War Measures Act in 1918. Restrictions on liquor sales lasted only a few years in most jurisdictions and liquor sales resumed in most provinces by the late 1920s. Quebec did not go dry, though Montreal restricted the number of permits it issued for "buvettes" (taprooms) after the Fédération nationale Saint-Jean-Baptiste women brought in a petition bearing sixty thousand signatures.[1] Although some jurisdictions, such as Windsor, Ontario, saw increased crime as a result of rum-running, alcohol-related crimes reportedly fell overall by more than half during prohibition. Alcohol consumption per capita dropped during prohibition by an estimated 40 percent. When prohibition ended, the sale of alcohol was taxed by government and new regulations meant tighter controls on the alcoholic content and on the availability of alcohol.

Single working women now spent their earnings at cinemas and at dance halls where live bands played. "Young people, be they English or French Canadian, Catholic, Protestant or Jewish, immigrants from Poland, Italy or Britain, moved together on the dance floor rewriting the social boundaries that constructed their daily lives," according to Tamara Myers in *Caught: Montreal's Modern Girls and the Law, 1869–1945*. Clubs were racially segregated, though some Montreal jazz clubs defied the taboo on racial mingling late in the 1930s.

In 1928, women participated for the first time at the Olympic summer games, establishing Canadian women's capability in competitive sports. Bobby Rosenfeld won a silver medal in the 100-metre sprint and a gold medal as a member of the women's relay team.

Women increased their participation in public life and continued to seek an expanded role for government in efforts to reduce the misery of the poor, the mentally ill, vulnerable children and the elderly. Due to women's successful efforts, mother's allowance programs to assist destitute women and their children had been enacted in most jurisdictions. Women pushed for expanded public health services, including well-baby clinics and in support of campaigns to reduce the spread of disease. Public health measures helped prove the effectiveness of spending tax money on public health care, and the federal government had taken women's advice and set up the Department of Health in 1919.

Generally, the political climate in the inter-war period was not conducive to social reforms. Between 1919 and 1936, the federal government cracked down on leftist causes, strikes were broken by mounted police, and non-British labour agitators were deported.[2] In 1937, Quebec Premier Maurice Duplessis' Padlock Law became an effective tool to quell labour and social unrest in Quebec, until the law was ruled unconstitutional in 1957.

Chinese immigration was curbed by Prime Minister Mackenzie King under the 1923 Chinese Exclusion Act. Chinese labourers were prohibited from most jobs and white women were prohibited from working for "Asiatic" men, who were viewed as promulgators of the opium and prostitution trades. Speaking against such laws, B.C. judge Helen Gregory MacGill told *Chatelaine* magazine in 1928 that an employer's race was not the problem. "What is needed," she said, "is protection against recognized danger, not restriction directed against a race."

WORK IN PROGRESS

In 1921, female workers aged fourteen and older made up 17 percent of the paid workforce.[3] Although most provinces had established minimum wage boards to reduce the economic exploitation of female workers, many female-dominated classes of employment were excluded, including domestic work, teaching and nursing. Also, few inspectors were hired to enforce labour laws. As a result, pieceworkers in the garment trades regularly complained they were not receiving the minimum wage, and employer fines, as little as $50 in Quebec, were not high enough to serve as a deterrent.

By the mid-1920s, domestic workers made up 20 percent of the female labour force. Domestic workers' work conditions had eased slightly as they were no longer required to live in their employers' homes, and a number of maids' organizations were formed.

While 12 percent of male workers were unionized, only 1 percent of female workers belonged to unions.[4] A male buttonhole maker in the 1920s could earn as much as $36 per week, while a female buttonhole maker could be paid just $22 per week. Most jobs in the garment industry remained segregated: men worked as higher paid cutters and pressers, and women did all of the work in between. As a result of these and other inequities, thousands of female members of the Industrial Union of Needle Trades Workers struck in 1931 in Toronto and 1934 in Montreal.

For the majority of female workers, low wages meant women lived with their families well after they entered the workforce. This included the more than 18 percent of the female workforce made up of clerical workers. There were 90,000 clerical workers in Canada in 1921, a jump of more than 55,000 in two decades.

Myths persisted that women didn't need to work and only did so for "pin money." And so the Toronto chapter of the Council of Women undertook a study of three hundred stenographers and secretaries in 1929 to determine women's motivations for working. Contrary to the view that women worked only until marriage, 79 percent of those surveyed were married. Of those married workers, 54 percent said their husbands had steady employment. A majority of women surveyed had children and 27 percent said they were working to pay off doctors' bills. Interestingly, when asked how long they intended to work, 52 percent said indefinitely, or as long as they were able.[5]

It was a time when employers, including public civil service commissions, still routinely classified such jobs by sex, reserving higher paid positions for men. Many employers barred married women from employment, a practice denounced by the Business and Professional Women's Club. Women worked out of necessity, yet female workers were required to demonstrate respectability in order to obtain employment. Department stores and domestic employers kept a watchful eye on female employees, firing them if they stepped outside of acceptable boundaries of female behaviour. Similarly, women applying for mother's allowance were required to prove their worthiness and respectability.

Professional women's organizations, including the Business and Professional Women's Club, the Federation of Medical Women of Canada, the Federation of Women Teachers' Associations of Ontario and the Canadian Nurses' Association, addressed low rates of pay and other employment issues. By the end of the 1920s, 23 percent of undergraduates and 35 percent of graduate students at Canadian universities were female. Women began to break many employment barriers, becoming pilots, scientists, politicians and university professors, although when the Depression hit, starting in 1929, there was a backlash against women holding jobs. At this time, the Council of Women antagonized many of its members when it distanced itself from backing women's right to work in all fields.

The number of nurses in Canada was 21,000 in 1921, and the number of female teachers was 50,000. For Quebec's female teachers, discrimination was particularly acute. In 1935, the minimum annual salary for female teachers in rural schools was $300, and some were paid less. It was "a time when the average Canadian renter paid $366 a year for shelter."[6]

Laure Gaudreault of La Malbaie, a town north of Quebec City, took up the cause of Quebec's female teachers in her role as a newspaper columnist. Gaudreault promoted the Fédération catholique des institutrices rurales, becoming its organizer in 1937. The organization slowly won pension increases and served as an inspiration for Quebec teachers' organizing efforts.

WOMEN IN POLITICS

By the early 1920s, women had been elected to legislative assemblies of B.C., Alberta, Saskatchewan and Manitoba. All of the women elected to provincial legislatures prior to the Second World War were from the western provinces.

In 1921, Mary Ellen Smith became Canada's first female cabinet minister after she joined the B.C. Liberals. First elected as an independent under the slogan "women and children first," in 1918, Smith won a by-election in a Vancouver riding represented by her husband, Ralph Smith, until his death. Although she was appointed a minister without portfolio, Smith introduced the province's first minimum wage law. Smith advocated for the appointment of women judges and supported measures to establish juvenile courts and welfare for deserted wives. In 1921, British Columbia introduced the first maternity leave legislation in Canada. The province's Maternity Protection Act of 1921 prohibited the employment of women for six weeks following childbirth and ensured women would not be fired during their leave.

Next door in Alberta, the United Farmers of Alberta (UFA) formed the government in 1921, and Irene Parlby soon became the second female cabinet minister in Canada. Parlby, a former president of the United Farm Women of Alberta, was an articulate advocate for women's legal and economic rights during her fourteen-year tenure as an MLA. The UFA government introduced eighteen bills aimed at improving the welfare of women and children, many of which were initiated by Parlby. They included laws to improve women's property rights, set minimum wages and protect children. In Alberta's 1921 election, Nellie McClung was elected to the legislature as a Liberal. She pushed for old-age pensions, increased rights for widows and improved factory conditions.

The federal election of December 6, 1921, the first in which women voted on the same basis as men, saw the election of Agnes Macphail, the first female member of Parliament, to the House of Commons. Macphail, a former school teacher, was elected under the Progressive Party banner, a party affiliated with the United Farmers of Ontario. She represented the Ontario riding of Grey Southeast and was subsequently re-elected as a United Farmers of Ontario-Labour Member of Parliament.

Canada's first female MP, Agnes Macphail, was a champion of prisoners, miners, farmers and women.

Canada's first federal female politician described her first session in Parliament as "miserable," since most of her fellow MPs scorned her. When one of her critics shouted at her "Don't you wish you were a man?" Macphail shot back, "Don't you?"[7]

Macphail was described by Susan E. Merritt in her book, *Herstory: Women from Canada's Past* as a "a warm outgoing thirty-one-year-old" who liked to dance and had multiple suitors. But she was nonetheless characterized by the press as a "cantankerous old maid." "Determined" might have been a more accurate way to describe the politician who, for fourteen of her nineteen years in Ottawa, remained Canada's lone female MP. Like other female politicians of the era, Macphail fought for social and legal reforms to aid women and the underprivileged.

Her concerns included old-age pensions, increased funding for schools and public health care, the creation of unemployment insurance and programs in aid of farmers. "It is true that the farmers work hard," Macphail once said, "it is true that their days are long and their pay is poor. But it is also infinitely true that the farm woman's day is longer and her pay poorer."

Macphail was a pacifist. In 1929, she became the first Canadian woman appointed to the League of Nations in Geneva. In the mid-1920s, Macphail, along with other progressive-minded MPs, formed the Ginger Group, a coalition of labour, farm and independent MPs. They were among the founders of the Co-operative Commonwealth Federation in Calgary in 1932. One of the CCF's goals was the creation of the modern welfare state, envisioned to include unemployment insurance, universal pensions and national health insurance (a precursor to medicare).

One of Macphail's greatest passions was prison reform. In the 1920s, shackling, beatings and long periods in solitary confinement were still common. Macphail successfully fought for the Archambault Royal Commission on Penal Reform in 1935, which investigated the conditions in Canada's prisons. She then fought for the implementation of its recommendations and helped establish the Elizabeth Fry Society in aid of female prisoners. Her efforts further paid off when unemployment insurance and family allowances were introduced in 1940.

Canada's second female MP, Martha Purdy Black, stepped into her ailing husband's former House of Commons seat in the 1935 election. Black had become a successful businesswoman during the Klondike Gold Rush. She was an ardent proponent of improved pensions and measures to stem unemployment.

Elected in a 1940 by-election, Dorise Nielsen, a United Progressive

Party MP from Saskatchewan, was Canada's third female MP. Nielsen "introduced important discussion on equal pay, the protection of motherhood and infant care," according to Joan Sangster in *Dreams of Equality: Women on the Canadian Left 1920–1950*. An articulate speaker, Nielsen worked to bring attention to the plight of working women and farmers in the West. She also protested the internment of Japanese-Canadians and argued that Canada's new family allowance should be payable to the mother, not the father. Nielson, by then a single mother, frequently struggled to find suitable care for her children for the five years she sat in the Commons.

SUFFRAGE IN QUEBEC

Quebec suffragists had few political allies. The province's powerful bishops held that there was no basis in "natural law" for women to vote or participate in public life. The influential politician and founder of *Le Devoir* newspaper, Henri Bourassa, was a staunch opponent of female suffrage. "[It is] the introduction of feminism under its most noxious guise: the voter-woman, who will soon spawn the man-woman, that hybrid and repugnant monster who will kill the mother-woman and the wife-woman," Bourassa claimed.

In 1922, Marie Gérin-Lajoie, along with the Montreal Women's Club's Anna Lyman, headed a new organization, the Comité provincial pour le suffrage féminin (Provincial Suffrage Committee), to coordinate the efforts of Quebec suffrage supporters. The organization had two branches — one English, one French — and Lyman and Gérin-Lajoie were its co-presidents. Thérèse Casgrain, who would later lead the suffrage campaign in Quebec, was a founding member. Casgrain, McGill professor Carrie Derick and Idola Saint-Jean were among four hundred women at who travelled to Quebec City in 1922 to support a suffrage bill before government.

In 1927, Saint-Jean led the newly formed Alliance canadienne pour le vote des femmes au Quebec, which championed the vote among working-class women.[8] She also wrote on suffrage for newspapers and magazines. Saint-Jean ran as an independent candidate in the 1930 federal election. Compared to their counterparts in the rest of Canada, married women in Quebec at this time had fewer rights. A legal separation remained all but impossible for Quebec women. While a Quebec husband could obtain a legal separation if his wife was adulterous, a Quebec wife could only obtain a legal separation on the grounds of adultery if her husband's mistress resided in the family home. Under Quebec's Civil Code, women did not have control over their own earnings or have a say regarding the sale or disposal of family property.

Thérèse Casgrain assumed the leadership of the Provincial Suffrage Committee, renamed the League for Women's Rights in 1929. She led the group until 1942. Its objectives included amending Quebec's Civil Code to give women greater rights.

Elsewhere in Canada, the 1920s saw most legislatures pass legislation to give mothers an equal right to the custody and control of their children upon divorce. Women also secured a legal right to a share of marital property upon divorce; however, they were not entitled to financial support if they were adulterers. The 1930 Divorce Act of Ontario granted women the right to divorce on the same grounds as men — simple adultery. Previously, a woman could only obtain a divorce if her husband committed incestuous adultery, rape, sodomy, bestiality, bigamy or adultery coupled with cruelty or desertion. Most jurisdictions, with the exception of Quebec and Newfoundland, established provincial divorce courts during this time. Canada would not have a uniform federal divorce law until 1968.

A Quebec commission on women's civil rights, the 1929 Doiron

Commission, netted a few small improvements, including the right of women to keep their paycheques and maintain child custody upon separation. The commission concluded: "Women themselves have not really evolved. Created to be the companions of men, women are always, and above all else, wives and mothers."

Quebec women, who had repeatedly petitioned the Quebec Assembly for the vote, turned to King George V in 1935 and to Ottawa in 1938 for support. On April 25, 1940, a bill for the enfranchisement of women was finally passed by Quebec's Liberal government.

THE PERSONS CASE

In 1916, Emily Murphy, the first female magistrate in Canada, was presiding over an Edmonton court for women that she had lobbied to create. It was her first day on the job and the defence counsel, Eardley Jackson, while defending his client on bootlegging charges, charged that Murphy was not qualified as a magistrate because women were not persons under the terms of the British North America Act.

An Alberta court ruled that there was no disqualification for women magistrates, and a few years after women won the right to vote and stand for election, Murphy started a lobby to end the all-male Senate. The National Council of Women threw in its support. At a conference of the Federated Women's Institutes of Canada in 1919, presided over by Murphy, delegates passed a resolution calling on the prime minister to appoint a female senator. Over the next few years, members of the National Council of Women wrote letters to Prime Minister Mackenzie King urging him to appoint Murphy to the Senate. However, each time a Senate seat became open, women's hopes were dashed as another male senator was appointed.

After lobbying King unsuccessfully for many years, Murphy changed her tactics. Murphy's brother, a lawyer, advised her of a legal provision that would permit her to petition Ottawa to seek an Order in Council asking the Supreme Court for a legal interpretation of the law as it related to the appointment of senators. It would avoid a costly court case and all that was required to initiate the process was five petitioners. The four women who joined Murphy's quest were high-profile Alberta feminists who, along with Murphy, became known as the Famous Five. Henrietta Muir Edwards, who in 1875 had founded the Working Girls' Association in Montreal, was the convenor of laws for the National Council of Women for thirty-eight years. Nellie McClung, Louise McKinney and Irene Parlby were all former or present Alberta MLAs.

Their case seemed like a mere formality. After all, Parliament clearly considered women to be "qualified persons" under Section 41 of the BNA Act when it allowed them to run for election to the House of Commons. And yet, prime ministers Robert Borden, Arthur Meighen and William Lyon Mackenzie King had declined to appoint a woman to the Senate. Justice Department staff held that since the original framers of Section 24 of the BNA Act had not intended to include women in the eligibility criteria for the Senate, they were not eligible in the present day. In 1921, Edmund Newcombe, a Department of Justice official who was later appointed to the Supreme Court, advised government: "In the absence of any precise authority to the contrary, I hold they are not qualified. There is no Latin word to describe a Senatress."[9]

The Person's Case was thus launched in 1927. The question for the Supreme Court petition was eventually decided by justice officials to be: Does the word "person" in section 24 of the British North America Act, 1867, include female persons? Murphy initially opposed the Justice Department's focus on the definition of persons. She was all too aware that British common law held that women were persons in "matters of pains and penalties, but not in matters of rights and privileges."

On April 28, 1928, the Supreme Court of Canada ruled unanimously that women were not qualified persons to be appointed to the Senate of Canada. Undaunted, Murphy immediately encouraged the deputy minister of Justice to appeal the case to the Judicial Committee of the British Privy Council. The case was represented by Newton Rowell, a former Ontario Liberal MP in Robert Borden's Union government. Rowell had also represented the female petitioners before the Supreme Court. His granddaughter, Nancy Ruth, would be appointed to the Senate in 2005.

A year and a half later, on October 18, 1929, the British Privy Council ruled unanimously in the case officially known as Edwards *v.* Canada that women were persons according to the BNA Act and were therefore qualified to be appointed to the Senate of Canada. The ruling in the Persons Case was written by Lord Chancellor John Sankey. It was the first time Sankey had presided at the Judicial Committee of the Privy Council, and the case became a historic ruling. In it, Sankey invoked the concept of a constitution as a "living tree" that grows with time to reflect social customs. It was this concept that, fifty years later, would inform the creation of Canada's Charter of Rights and Freedoms.

Four months following the Persons ruling, in February 1930, King appointed Cairine Wilson to the Red Chamber. Canada's first female senator had been active in the Victorian Order of Nurses, the Young Women's Christian Association and the National Federation of Liberal Women of Canada. Wilson took up the cause of divorce liberalization and, in 1938, spoke out against the Munich Agreement's appeasement of German Chancellor Adolph Hitler. Wilson was one of the few Canadian politicians (Agnes Macphail was another) who protested Canada's restrictive immigration policies that prevented Jews fleeing persecution from entering Canada. In 1949, Wilson would become Canada's first female delegate to the United Nations General Assembly.

On the fiftieth anniversary of the Persons Case in 1979, Governor General Ed Schreyer created the Governor General's Awards in Commemoration of the Persons Case to recognize individuals who have made a long-standing contribution to the equality of women in Canada. A monument of the Famous Five stands on Parliament Hill. Murphy, a life-long conservative, did not realize her dream of becoming a Senator. It was not only her political ties that were held against her. King had once commented that Murphy was "a little too masculine and perhaps a bit too flamboyant."

Murphy later became a controversial figure due to her support for eugenics, a philosophy that billed itself as the science for improving the human race through controlled breeding. Eugenics was a popular idea, even among progressives, in the early twentieth century and many countries had sterilization programs. It was believed by eugenics supporters that if the family size of those with the lowest intelligence were limited, the overall intelligence of society would rise. Such arguments were also used to gain support for legalized birth control, since reducing the family size of the poor was seen as a way to reduce "mental defectiveness," which was believed to be hereditary. Some eugenics supporters cast issues like sexually transmitted diseases, prostitution, delinquency and unwed pregnancy as primarily matters of "moral laxity."

Murphy, though never elected to public office, endorsed Alberta's sterilization program for the "feeble-minded," introduced in 1928 by the United Farmers of Alberta government. She died in 1933, the year Tommy Douglas's master's thesis, entitled "The Problems of the Subnormal Family," outlined a national eugenics program under which couples would need to be declared morally and mentally fit before marrying. Under the future Saskatchewan premier's imagined program, those with low intelligence or moral laxity would be sent to state-run farms to be reformed, while those found to be mentally defective would be sterilized. Eugenics lost its favour among social progressives, including Douglas, after German Chancellor Adolph Hitler adopted the idea of improving the human race through selective breeding.

A total of 2,822 women and men in Alberta were subjected to coerced and forced sterilization in Alberta; most of them were female residents in institutions for the mentally ill. Many women in B.C. and Ontario were also sterilized without their consent and Aboriginal women were disproportionately sterilized. In some cases, poor women seeking abortions in Canada were asked by doctors if they would agree to be sterilized if granted an abortion. The most vociferous opponents of forced sterilizations were women, including Leilani Muir, who won a landmark legal case in 1996 for wrongful sterilization and confinement in Alberta, where the practice ended in 1972.[10]

SOCIAL WELFARE

The rise of the welfare state was a hallmark of the inter-war years. The new Department of Health had been established in 1919 to emphasize sanitation, vaccination, disease control and the development of healthy children. A number of reform-minded MPs were also elected. As a result, increased demands for greater public aid for the elderly and disabled, war widows, the unemployed, the sick and the destitute were heard in the House of Commons.

In 1925, Liberal leader Mackenzie King, in exchange for the support of the Progressive Party, promised to introduce legislation on old-age pensions. In 1927, the bill that would later become the

Old Age Pension Act, was first introduced. MP Agnes Macphail, was among those who worked to draft the bill. At first, pensions provided $20 per month to those over seventy years of age who had lived in Canada for twenty or more years, were British subjects and passed a means test.

Most jurisdictions had separate courts and jails for juveniles, and wayward juveniles could be streamed into training facilities instead of jails. In practice, many of the facilities bore all of the hallmarks of prisons. Juvenile courts were created to discipline delinquent minors and keep them out of adult prisons. Young women found working in prostitution were usually sent to a training or reform school. In Montreal, there were separate juvenile delinquency institutions for French Canadians, English Quebeckers and delinquent Jewish girls.

An early proponent of child welfare laws, Charlotte Whitton became an outspoken public figure shortly after obtaining her M.A. from Queens University in 1918. Whitton had been the star of her university women's hockey team and was the first female editor of the student newspaper, the *Queens Journal.* In 1920, Whitton was hired as director of the Canadian Council on Child Welfare. She was also convenor of the standing committee on child welfare for the National Council of Women, which urged local councils to lobby for recreational programs for children. Their aim was to prevent delinquency and to press Ottawa to adhere to international child labour conventions.

Whitton, a popular public speaker on child welfare reform, wanted Canada to stop bringing children into the country to work as domestics. Politically conservative, Whitton supported equal pay for women but not liberalized divorce. In one of the many reports she was commissioned to write, Whitton disparaged Manitoba's "white trash" population and documented stories of children forced by their parents to beg or steal. Citing stories of children living in violent and neglected environments, Whitton urged provinces to enact laws to remove maltreated children from their parents care. Slowly, networks of social workers were employed by government agencies to control wayward

Charlotte Whitton was the first woman to become mayor of a major Canadian city, Ottawa, in 1951.

children and teenagers. According to *Saturday Night* magazine, "[Whitton] has elevated social welfare from the abyss of common charity to the standards of a profession."[11]

Whitton was later an advisor on Ottawa's federal unemployment relief policy. A woman of humour and passion, she was known for her fierce approach to her adversaries. She once punched a civic official who insulted her. It has been speculated that Whitton and her lifelong companion Margaret Grier, a federal civil servant, were in an intimate relationship. Whitton lived with until Grier until her death in 1947, and the two were regarded as a couple by many of their friends. Some sources claim their relationship was simply a "Boston marriage," a relationship between two women who have merely an abiding friendship.

In 1951, Whitton became the first female mayor of a major Canadian city when Ottawa City Council unanimously elected her to the interim post upon the death of Mayor Grenville Goodwin. Whitton served as Ottawa mayor from 1951 to 1956 and from 1960 to 1964. She once famously said: "Whatever women do, they must do it twice as well as men to be thought half as good. Luckily, this is not difficult."

Barbara Hanley became the first female mayor in Canada in 1936 when she was elected mayor of Webbwood, Ontario.

THE GREAT DEPRESSION

During the Depression, the wages of girls and women became more critical to their families as the industries in which male workers were concentrated, including resource extraction and agriculture, suffered huge employment declines.

By 1933, 28 percent of the workforce in Canada was unemployed and two million people were on relief. In many urban Ontario centres, many women found work as telephone operators, office workers, sales clerks, waitresses and hotel launderers, according to Katrina Srigley, author of *Breadwinning Daughters*. Of the women in the Toronto workforce, 72 percent were between ages fifteen and thirty-five, and most were single. Since women were commonly fired upon marriage, many women could simply not afford to get married during the Depression, according to Srigley. Clerical workers earned $12.50 a week, a rate of pay similar to what men in relief camps were initially paid. Women in textiles earned $12.41 per week in 1934. Male textile workers were paid $17.31 per week, 40 percent more.

The overall scarcity of jobs placed added pressure on women to have sex in exchange for job security. *Hugh* magazine, reputed for articles criticizing employers who took advantage of female employees, wrote that the working girl "will find no lack of offers of employment from men who make it clear they like to be rewarded with services of an intimate nature." Srigley concluded that "the economic conditions of the decade forced a good number of women into undignified employment."

Many women had to find work since public relief and work programs did not initially include them. Some Black and immigrant women in Toronto reportedly accepted work as live-in domestics for as little as $25 per month. At Eaton's, piecework rates for dresses were reduced from $5 per dozen before the 1929 market crash, to $1.35 per dozen by 1934. Many women experienced wage cuts of 70 percent and women often worked in solidarity with each other. In Toronto, when members of the International Ladies Garment Workers' Union struck Eaton's in 1934, members of the Toronto Local Council of Women raised funds for the strikers and joined the picket line.

A report to the national Price Spreads Commission in 1934 quoted a witness named Miss A. Tucker as saying that "the girls were just about insane. In fact, it got to such a climax that they were threatening to commit suicide and even I myself was contemplating the same thing."[12]

A six-week Montreal strike in 1934 saw Jewish and French Canadian female textile workers who walked out come under attack by mounted police. They were said to have pricked the horses on which police rode with hair pins, causing the horses to throw their riders. Before the strike was over, the Quebec Minimum Wage Commission had increased wages for female operatives and reduced their work week from fifty-five to forty-eight hours. In 1937, a strike by Montreal garment workers from different ethnic and linguistic backgrounds resulted in a 10 percent wage increase, a new forty-four-hour work week and the promise of a closed (union-only) shop.

The Canadian Federation of Business and Professional Women's Clubs, which included office workers, bank workers and other white-collar workers, passed a resolution in 1931 affirming women's right to work regardless of their marital status. According to Ruth A. Frager and Carmela Patrias, authors of *Discounted Labour: Women Workers in Canada, 1870–1939*, Vancouver women grew more determined during this era: "Depression-era conditions radicalized workers and drew more women workers into labour organizations and strikes than in any previous period."

Male workers had shown little interest in office work, domestic work, sewing or telephone operation, but in 1933, Médéric Martin, a member of the Quebec Legislative Assembly, proposed that women be forced to cede their jobs to male relatives. Several politicians in English Canada also called for women to be fired so that men could have their jobs. The Canadian Catholic Confederation of Labour, which represented many female textile workers, petitioned the Quebec government to bar all women from working for wages, except in case of "absolute necessity."

Quebec women continued to be thwarted in their equality efforts by the government and the Catholic Church. The prime purpose of Quebec women was to ensure the survival of French Canadian society by having an abundance of children, it was claimed. Voting and the consequent participation of women in public life would crush Quebec's birth rate. Women's rights leader, Thérèse Casgrain, refuted such arguments, countering that "women's special qualifies made them particularly qualified to select their political representatives."[13]

Of the 826,000 Canadians who were out of work during the Depression, an estimated 20 percent were women. Minority women experienced overt discrimination. Women of British heritage were almost exclusively hired for office work. Until the Second World War, Winnipeg's Eaton's routinely relegated Jewish women to behind-the-scenes work in the mail-order department. Immigrant women and women of colour simply weren't hired during the Depression. Toronto want ads routinely requested domestic workers by ethnic specifications, such as Russian, Polish or Negro. "As one African Canadian woman recalled, 'We weren't allowed to go into factory work until Hitler started the war.'"[14]

During the Depression years, white supremacist groups with anti-Semitic, anti-communist leanings arose. Ku Klux Klan cross burnings to spurn inter-racial marriage led to some arrests; however, sentences for Klan members were light. Immigrants who had been in Canada fewer than five years faced deportation if they went on relief — public aid that mostly took the form of rent and food vouchers. People who wanted relief had to give up any luxury items they owned, such as cars and telephones.

In Vancouver, the Local Council of Women organized training programs and aid for unemployed women, and took out newspaper advertisements encouraging employers to hire more women. Professional associations of women teachers fought for increased pay and the right to work while married, while female social workers discussed strategies to combat sex discrimination at work.

Militancy characterized women's role as consumers during this time. In 1932, Jewish women in Toronto organized to boycott kosher butchers who were charging inflated prices. Throughout the Depression, women actively protested inadequate relief policies. One of the largest demonstrations came on Mother's Day 1935, when women demonstrated in a Vancouver protest against relief camps.

Unemployment insurance came about at the recommendation of the Royal Commission on Dominion-Provincial Relations, which had been set up in 1937. Newton Wesley Rowell, the lawyer who had argued the Person's Case in 1929, was the Royal Commission's first chairperson. The Commission recommended that the federal government take over control of unemployment insurance and pensions. It also recommended the creation of equalization payments — transfers of money from the federal government to the province — each year.

Women and the Wage Gap

Earning Comparison for Univeristy-Educated Workers (2014)
Source: CCPA

$1.00

$0.82
(Public sector)

$0.73
(Private sector)

Earning Comparison for Hourly-Wage Workers (2013)
Source: Statistics Canada

$1.00

$0.86

Earning Comparison for All Workers
Source: Statistics Canada

$1.00

$0.72
(2013)

$0.64
(1981)

Senior Management Positions by Gender (2009)
Source: Statistics Canada

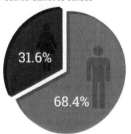

31.6%

68.4%

Average Annual Earnings (2011)
Source: Statistics Canada

$47,100

$31,100

Workforce Participation of Women Aged 25-54
Source: Statistics Canada

77.6%
(2012)

48.7%
(1976)

BIRTH CONTROL

The economic hardship of the Depression spurred a drop in Canada's birth rate. Infant mortality rates improved and women had an average of 2.8 births compared to 3.3 five years earlier. In the early 1930s, however, maternal deaths still accounted for 10 to 15 percent of all deaths among women in their child-bearing years.

With birth control illegal and unavailable to many women, thousands of women died from complications from abortions. Women often relied on home remedies for contraception that were unreliable or dangerous. Doctors were still in the habit of telling women that their "safe" period (when they were unlikely to conceive) was the middle of their monthly cycle, while advertisements in women's magazines hinted that disinfectant products had contraceptive qualities when used in a post-coital douche.

Desperate for advice on family planning, many Canadian women wrote to Margaret Sanger, the well-known American family planning pioneer who first coined the term "birth control." A popular speaker, publisher and author, Sanger had been jailed for distributing birth control information to immigrant women in New York. As well as touting family planning, Sanger was adamant that the entitlement of women to sexual pleasure was integral to their empowerment. Russian-born anarchist anarchist Emma Goldman lived at various times in Canada and was a proponent of birth control. Dubbed by Edgar Hoover to be "the most dangerous woman in America," Goldman filled Toronto lecture halls with her talks on topics that included birth control, women's rights, communism and anarchism.

It was a time when "few doctors would fit an unmarried woman with a diaphragm. Condoms, which were associated with prostitution, were available at select pharmacies or illegal vendors."[15] It has been estimated that four thousand women in Canada died from botched abortions between 1926 and 1946. This figure represents one in five of the 21,000 maternal deaths that occurred in Canada during this period.[16]

Canada's 1892 law on birth control and abortion in the Criminal Code stated that, "everyone is guilty of an indictable offence and liable to two years imprisonment who knowingly without lawful justification or excuse offers to sell, advertise, publishes an advertisement or has for sale or disposal any means or instructions or any medicine, drug or article intended or represented as a means of preventing conception or of causing abortion or miscarriage."

The Birth Control League of Canada, founded in 1923, was inspired by a cross-Canada tour by Margaret Sanger. Violet McNaughton, women's page editor of the *Western Producer*, supported farm women who argued that the health of women and children would be improved if family size were limited. Women grasped the political importance of controlling fertility. According to "A.P.," a contributor in the *Western Producer*, "Women can have no freedom or equality until they own their own bodies. A woman should not become a mother except through her own choice."[17]

In 1929, the women's branch of the United Farmers of Canada, Saskatchewan chapter, became the first women's organization to call on Ottawa to rescind its ban on birth control information and devices. Delegates also called for the establishment of public birth control clinics.

A labour women's conference in Winnipeg in 1930 was a forum where Brandon, Manitoba, birth control advocate Beatrice Brigden championed voluntary motherhood. Brigden lectured across Canada and counselled women on birth control on behalf of the Methodist Church Department of Social Service and Evangelism. She was part of the social gospel movement that stemmed from Canada's evangelical

Protestant churches. The social gospel critique of Canadian capitalism at the end of the First World War favoured social reconstruction and the dismantling of capitalism's excesses. Methodists envisioned a new cooperative social order and the movement propelled many into politics. Brigden was a founder of the Co-operative Commonwealth Federation.

Things changed in 1929 when Alvin R. Kaufman, owner of Kaufman Rubber Company, established the Parents Information Bureau in Kitchener, Ontario. Throughout the Depression, the bureau was staffed by fifty women, many of them nurses, who counselled women on birth control and distributed contraceptive devices — mostly condoms and spermicidal jellies. Boldly, the women went door to door, often in poor areas, to discuss family planning and sell contraceptives. More than 120,000 orders were placed for contraceptive supplies.

In 1936, one of the bureau's staff, social worker Dorothea Palmer, was arrested for violating the Criminal Code prohibition on birth control. Her offence had taken place in the predominantly French community of Eastview, Ontario, where 25 percent of the population was on welfare or relief. "A woman should be master of her own body," Palmer told policemen during her interrogation.[18] After a six-month trial, Palmer was acquitted after she successfully argued that birth control was medically necessary.

By 1932, Canada's first birth control clinics had opened in B.C. and Hamilton, Ontario. Dr. Elizabeth Bagshaw, who graduated from the Women's Medical College in Toronto in 1905, operated a Hamilton clinic, which provided condoms, jellies, pessaries (a device inserted in the vagina to prevent pregnancy) and diaphragms for thirty-four years. Bagshaw sometimes performed abortions. Most of Bagshaw's medical experience was in obstetrics and over her career she attended more than three thousand births.[19] She continued her medical practice while operating the birth control clinic, where she served in an unpaid capacity until 1966. "Reviled at the time as a whore and a harlot and an agent of Satan, Dr. Bagshaw lived to be appointed a Member of the Order of Canada in 1973," according to Penney Kome, author of *Women of Influence: Canadian Women and Politics.* When she was forty-five, Bagshaw, who did not marry, adopted a son. Only reluctantly did Bagshaw retire, at age ninety-five.[20]

Dr. Elizabeth Bagshaw was the director of Hamilton's Birth Control Society Clinic when it opened in 1932.

The birth rate of Quebec women continued to be higher than the rest of Canada. Quebec women, who comprised 27 percent of Canadian women during the inter-war period, produced about 35 percent of children born. This includes approximately 2,500 children born out of wedlock per year in Quebec during this period.[21] Shame and a lack of economic resources led many young girls to homes for unwed mothers, which also functioned as orphanages. In one home, 47 percent of women had been previously employed as domestic workers. In homes operated by nuns, pregnant women were charged room and board and required to work at the facility after giving birth to pay off their debt, which included adoption fees and medical exams.

In spite of Quebec's Catholic culture, abortionists in the province rarely faced charges unless a patient died from an infection or other complication after admission to a hospital. According to Andrée Levesque, author of *Making and Breaking the Rules: Women in Quebec 1919–1933*, fifty-five abortionists were convicted in Quebec between 1919 and 1939. One third of those convicted were women. Those convicted tended to be repeat offenders and faced jail terms ranging from fifteen months to more than five years. Lay practitioners charged between $25 and $50 for an abortion, an amount that exceeded the weekly wage of many women. A physician-performed abortion cost $200.

7

THE SECOND WORLD WAR ERA, 1940–1959

German Chancellor Adolph Hitler had an agenda that was not only race driven but was built upon on the subjugation of women. At the International Council of Women triennial meeting in Stockholm, Sweden, in 1934, the German National Council of Women announced that it would disband rather than agree to swear allegiance to Hitler. It also refused to ban Jewish women from its affiliate organizations and refused to accept the appointment of Nazi women to leading positions within the organization.[1]

By the time Canada declared war on Germany in 1939, many Canadians believed that their country's involvement in the war was justified. A minority, including many women, held the view that war was unjustifiable under any circumstances. Regardless of women's views on the war, women in Canada were irrevocably affected by it. As members of the workforce in war-related industries, as members of the armed forces and as volunteers, women's involvement in public life became more visible.

VOLUNTEER CORPS

A year after Canada declared war on Germany in 1939, seven thousand Canadian women were enrolled in volunteer organizations in aid of the war effort. One of the largest organizations, led by Joan B. Kennedy of Victoria, was the British Columbia Women's Service Corps. Others included the Women's Volunteer Reserve Corps of Montreal, also known as the Canadian Beavers, as well as the French-speaking Corps de réserve national féminin and the Réserve canadienne féminine. These volunteers were taught military transport, map reading, first aid, motor mechanics and firefighting. Women's service corps lobbied Ottawa to form official women's auxiliary services for the armed forces, believing that their members would make excellent recruits. Independently, women's service clubs provided sleeping quarters and meals for women in service and packaged comforts like magazines and cigarettes for those serving overseas.

Then, in 1941, the Department of National War Services established the Women's Voluntary Service Division to coordinate women's involvement in projects such as recycling scrap metals, animal bones, rubber and glass. Women were also targets of campaigns to encourage the re-use of paper and even the collection of fats to be used for munitions. As homemakers, women were called upon to prevent waste and save and collect materials that could be recycled for use in war production. One poster encouraged women to "Dig In and Dig Out the Scrap." Local women's voluntary divisions distributed ration cards, trained volunteer staff to work in day nurseries, promoted war bonds and encouraged women to sew, knit and prepare "ditty bags" for servicemen and servicewomen overseas. Women's Institutes helped farm wives and daughters assume control of farm work in the absence of farm husbands and sons. Farm women drove tractors, made hay, picked fruit, raised gardens and increased the country's poultry and egg production.

WOMEN IN WAR INDUSTRIES

Necessity demanded that women step into jobs traditionally held by men and they did so in droves. Women not only replaced male workers who had enlisted, but they filled a growing demand for new workers in burgeoning war-related industries.

To facilitate women's entry into male bastions such as the aircraft industry, the federal government actively solicited and trained female workers to do work that many had formerly believed women incapable of doing. Jobs like building instrument panels for fighter planes, once viewed as precision work suitable only for highly skilled men, was suddenly spun as work that was well suited to the nimble hands and patient mind of a woman.

Between 1939 and 1945, the number of women in the Canadian workforce nearly doubled, from 638,000 to 1,077,000.[2] In munitions factories in Ontario and Quebec, some 44,000 women were employed, and another 33,000 were employed in the aircraft industry, which had the largest proportion of female workers of the wartime industries. Across Canada, 261,000 women worked in industries linked to wartime needs. In all, a third of Canadian females aged fifteen and older were employed by 1944. These figures do not include women employed in farming, a sector that also saw an increase in the number of female workers.

By 1942, twenty-one national women's organizations had lent their support to the National Selective Service (NSS) program, established to recruit women into the labour force during wartime. At first, the NSS targeted only single women, but it later recruited childless married women and then recruited married women with children. Many of the skilled jobs were well paid, although women were not paid at the same rates as men. Close to half of all participants in pre-employment training through the NSS were women, and their work included welding, aircraft assembly, shipbuilding, electronics, drafting and industrial chemistry.

To facilitate the entry of mothers into war-related industries, federal-provincial child-care agreements, initiated by the federal government in 1942, saw twenty-eight day nurseries established in Ontario and five in Quebec. The day nurseries, which oversaw 2,500 children, were staffed by paid workers trained in the psychology and care of children. At first, the day nurseries were restricted to children of mothers in war-related industries. However, after extensive lobbying by women, Ontario and Quebec amended their Wartime Day Nurseries Agreements in 1944 to include children of all working mothers, according to Ruth Roach Pierson in her book *They're Still Women After All*.

Patriotism was the focus of recruitment campaigns aimed to draw women into the non-traditional areas of work. Interestingly, women's motives didn't always match those of government propagandists. As Pierson documented, "Fifty percent of the women were working full time out of economic need; some were widows without, or with very small pensions; others were deserted and unmarried mothers; still others had husbands who were unemployed or ill or earning inadequate wages." A further 30 percent were working to "help husbands pay off debts, purchase homes or get re-established in business. Fifteen percent were working part-time to supplement family incomes."[3] Fewer than 10 percent of women in war-related industries in said their main motivation was patriotic.

Margaret Grier, a social worker and civil servant whose background included working in juvenile courts, was appointed assistant associate director of the National Selective Service and was responsible for administering the Dominion-Provincial Wartime Day Nurseries Agreement. At the end of the war, Grier tried to convince the federal government to continue to finance day nurseries. However, the federal government ceased funding day nurseries.

A graduate of the University of Toronto's electrical engineering program in 1927, Elsie Gregory MacGill was the first woman in North America to earn a degree as an aeronautical engineer. She was also the first woman to design an airplane — the Maple Leaf Trainer II. MacGill completed her doctorate in aeronautical engineering at the Massachusetts Institute of Technology and, just before her graduation, contracted polio, after which time she walked with the assistance of metal canes. During the war, MacGill, in the position of chief aeronautical engineer at Canadian Car and Foundry, oversaw 4,500 workers involved in the production of 1,400 Hawker Hurricane fighter planes for the Royal Air Force. MacGill, a celebrated media example of women's contribution to the war effort, was dubbed "Queen of the Hurricanes." Following the war, MacGill became the first woman to work as a technical advisor for the United Nations International Aviation Organization. She was also president of the Canadian Federation of Business and Professional Women's Clubs and, in 1969, was appointed a member of the Royal Commission on the Status of Women.[4]

WOMEN IN THE ARMED FORCES

Canadian nurses had served in the First World War; however, the Second World War marked the first time women were uniformed for a wide variety of armed forces positions.

Between 1941 and 1945, 21,624 women were accepted into the Canadian Women's Army Corps (CWAC), a division of the military that trained women to serve in support roles to enable more men

"This is OUR battle too"

Join- CANADIAN WOMEN'S ARMY CORPS

Second World War recruitment ad for the Canadian Women Army Corps shows women in both traditional and non-traditional occupations.

to participate in fighting units. At first, CWAC was not part of the armed forces and, as such, its rank designations and insignias did not follow army practice. In 1942, Ottawa integrated CWAC into the armed forces and CWAC members trained as clerks, cooks, typists, quartermasters, telephone operators and drivers. Most trained in Kitchener, Ontario. As the war's end grew nearer and as more men were called upon for combat, servicewomen were trained in a greater number of technical trades. They trained in ciphering and decoding, vehicle maintenance, parachute rigging and signalling. Mary Greyeyes from the Muskeg Lake Reservation in Saskatchewan was the first Aboriginal woman to enlist in CWAC in 1942.[5] There were seventy Aboriginal women enlisted by the end of the war.

Another 17,030 women served in the Women's Division of the Royal Canadian Air Force, established in July 1941, while 7,043 served in the Women's Royal Canadian Naval Service (WRCNS, known as Wrens), established in July 1942. There were 4,473 nurses enlisted, a majority attached to the army, as well as thirty-eight female doctors.[6]

In 1943, after several months of complaints from enlisted women and women's organizations, the pay rate for service women was increased from two-thirds that of servicemen of equivalent rank to four-fifths. The policy change also allowed women to qualify to claim a dependent allowance for mothers, fathers and siblings; there were no allowances permitted for dependent husbands or children of servicewomen.

Five Canadian female pilots joined Britain's Air Transport Auxiliary, where they flew transport planes and ferried military aircraft from factories to bases. There were 166 women pilots in the auxiliary from around the world. Remarkably, the women were paid the same as male pilots of equal rank. Although restricted to non-combat roles, female pilots eventually learned to fly aircraft used by the British RAF and Fleet Air Arm, including Spitfires, Hurricanes and Mosquitoes. Some seventeen Canadian women serviced as wireless operators, or "sparks" during and after the war on foreign vessels. Most sparks served in the Norwegian navy.

And yet, as N.E.S. Griffiths wrote in *The Splendid Vision: Centennial History of the National Council of Women 1893–1993*, "To a very large extent, the women who entered the Canadian armed forces were seen by the military as support, rather than as operational personnel, and as replacements for men rather than as recruits in their own right."

The mottos of the three women's armed services embodied this support role. The Royal Canadian Air Force Women's Division had the slogan, "We Serve That Men May Fly." Likewise, that of the Wrens, or the Women's Royal Canadian Naval Service, was "We Serve That Men May Fight," while CWAC's slogan was "We Are the Women Behind the Men Behind the Guns."

Positioning women in support roles to men was likely a strategic move aimed to mitigate the public backlash that arose to women joining the war effort. According to surveys at the time, only 7 percent of Canadians thought that joining the armed forces was the best way for women to demonstrate their support for Canada's war effort.[7] Younger women, as well as enlisted servicemen and servicewomen tended to be more supportive. According to the Canadian War Museum, many people believed that women who joined the armed services were "loose" and had low moral standards.

"Wearing a uniform, marching, standing at attention and saluting were traditionally masculine behaviour," according to historian Ruth Roach Pierson. "The woman who behaved so appeared unconventional, 'unwomanly' and it was thus easy to assume that she would have broken with moral convention as well."

And yet, with thousands of young men and women working in close proximity to one another, it is not surprising that many servicemen and servicewomen became sexually involved. In order to reduce the spread of sexually transmitted diseases (STDs), a venereal disease control division was established. In 1941, the director-general of medical services recommended that members of CWAC who contracted syphilis or gonorrhea should be discharged from duty on medical grounds. Affected servicemen, however, received treatment for their STDs and continued to serve. "Some medical officials," wrote Ruth Roach Pierson, author of *They're Still Women After All: The Second World War and Canadian Womanhood*, "favoured discharge for servicewomen because VD was a greater cause for shame in women."[8]

In 1942, CWAC was integrated into the armed forces, and a small measure of equality came when the policy was to provide the same treatment for servicewomen who had acquired a venereal disease as enlisted men. By 1943, penicillin had been discovered and treatment of venereal disease improved. While education in prophylactic use was provided to enlisted men (along with an allotment of three condoms per month), women were not encouraged to use prophylactics, apparently out of a fear that it would cause a backlash if it were discovered back home.[9]

Throughout the war, the National Council of Women backed servicewomen's demands for increased pay and benefits, and remained unrelenting in its support for women to be trained in all trades and professions. The head of CWAC from 1940 until 1944 was Elizabeth Smellie, the first woman to gain the rank of colonel in the Canadian armed forces. Later, Joan B. Kennedy assumed the job of director of CWAC. Colonel Margaret Eaton served as director-general of CWAC in 1944.

By the end of the war, 45,000 women had enlisted in the Canadian Armed Forces where they made up 4.3 percent of those serving in Canada's war effort. By the end of the war in 1945, seventy-three servicewomen had lost their lives, according to Veterans Affairs.

JAPANESE INTERNMENT

By 1934, 6,500 Japanese women and 25,000 Japanese men had immigrated to Canada, settling mainly in B.C.[10] Ottawa placed greater restrictions on female Japanese immigrants to discourage permanent Japanese settlement in Canada. Upon their arrival to Canada, Japanese-Canadian women commonly worked in businesses with their husbands or ran their own dress shops. They also ran boarding houses or worked at lumbering, fishing or mining camps.

"To achieve their dreams, nay, to merely survive, they had to do harsh work for long hours both inside and outside their home and still be conscientious wives and homemakers," wrote Midge Ayukawa in *Sisters or Strangers: Immigrant, Ethnic and Racialized Women in Canadian History*. In 1941, there were over fifty Japanese language schools in B.C. However, the schoolchildren's parents were not allowed to vote because B.C. law excluded those who were Asian. This included people of Chinese, Hindu and Indian descent. Almost two hundred men of Japanese descent had fought in the Canadian army during the First World War and, in 1931, these veterans became the first Japanese-Canadians to vote.

In January 1941, the Cabinet War Committee recommended that Japanese-Canadians not be allowed in the armed services, although some were already enlisted. The day after the bombing of Pearl Harbor in December 1941, Canada declared war on Japan, and soon ordered all males of Japanese descent between the ages eighteen and forty-five to be removed from a hundred-mile-wide zone along the coast of B.C. At the time, about half of the fishing licences for salmon belonged to people of Japanese descent, and it was feared by some that Japanese-Canadians would aid an invasion of Canada.

On February 24, 1942, the mass evacuation of Japanese-Canadians, most of whom were born in Canada or were naturalized citizens, was ordered under the War Measures Act. Approximately 21,000 Japanese-Canadians were forced to turn over property to the Custodian of Alien Property and sent to detention camps. Their homes, businesses and personal property and family belongings were liquidated. When the B.C. Security Commission forced Japanese Canadian men to road camps, women and children were put in camps in B.C., Alberta and Nova Scotia.

Muriel Kitagawa was a B.C. journalist who defended Japanese-Canadians during the internment. Kitagaw was a contributor to the Japanese Canadian newspaper, the *New Canadian,* in 1939. Kitagawa and her family were among those who left the province rather than face internment. They moved to Toronto. There, Kitagawa criticized the treatment of those interned and the government's refusal to compensate Japanese-Canadians following the war. Kitagawa also labelled the subsequent deportation of Japanese nationals a human rights violation.[11]

Other women who were critical of Canada's treatment of those interned included Constance Hayward, a graduate of international affairs at the London School of Economics. Hayward, a lecturer for the United Nations Society, worked closely with Senator Cairine Wilson, an opponent of the disenfranchisement and deportation of Japanese-Canadians. Following the Second World War, citizenship restrictions for those of Asian descent were loosened and Japanese-Canadians received the federal vote in 1948.

WOMEN IN POST-WAR CANADA

Women did not willingly give up their newfound freedoms after the war. In spite of the desire of many women to remain in the military, the federal government disbanded the Canadian Women's Army Corps in 1946 and stood down the women's services in the air force and navy.

A Labour Department survey on post-war working intentions found that 72 percent of women intended to stay in the workforce and half of married women workers wanted to keep working. But by September 1945, 80,000 female manufacturing workers had been laid off. Canada's Re-instatement in Civil Employment Act of 1942 provided that former service personnel must receive their pre-enlistment jobs with full seniority. Since many female veterans' work experience prior to their service was categorized as replacement or temporary, many female veterans did not benefit from the provision.[12]

Women were fired, or simply not hired. Women looking for work in the public service were hindered by the federal government's reinstated ban on married women in the civil service. The federal government did not rescind the ban until 1955.

The National Council of Women of Canada was appalled at the post-war treatment of women who had served during the war. Its president, Mrs. Edgar Drury Hardy, decried the notion that "after the war women will go back to the kitchen." The Council had proposed a program of vocational training for women. It also called for the appointment of women to public boards and commissions and for "well-qualified women" to be placed on bodies "concerned with peace terms and post-war reconstruction."

After the war, many had hoped Canada would open its doors to Jewish Holocaust survivors; however, Canada took in proportionately fewer Jewish immigrants than other western countries following the war. Some seventeen thousand Jewish Canadians served in the armed forces in the Second World War.

The National Council of Women of Canada also supported the establishment of a national plan of compulsory health insurance and improved benefits under the Unemployment Insurance Act. The umbrella organization also called for greater respect for the bargaining rights of unions. The council re-iterated "women's freedom to choose at what and where she will work," regardless of marital status.[13]

But women were shooed back to the kitchen. A 1944 report on post-war employment in Canada, the Weir Report, didn't address women's training and employment needs and in a parliamentary address that year, Saskatchewan MP Dorise Nielson mocked the workplace discrimination against women when the war ended: "Well, girls, you have done a nice job. You looked very cute in your overalls and we appreciate what you have done for us, but just run along; go home; we can get along without you very easily." One former servicewoman, writing in the *Canadian Home Journal* in April 1945, said that casting trained female workers aside was "like putting a chick back in the shell — it cannot be done without destroying spirit, heart or mind." Shut out of most employment and training programs, many married women became homemakers — some willingly, others due to a lack of employment options. Others used their earnings to go to university.

Marion Orr, who had been a Canadian pilot with the British Air Transport Auxiliary, sought opportunities to fly after the war. "I felt so empty," she recalled, "It was like my whole life was behind me. I knew I'd never be near a military airfield again and never get a chance to fly those fast planes."[14] After studying aeromechanics, Orr eventually opened her own flying school in Barker Field, Ontario.

The federal government discouraged married women from working by penalizing their husbands. Income tax regulations were changed so that married women could earn just $250 annually before their husbands could no longer claim a full married status exemption. During the war, the amount had been $750. Picking up on a recommendation in the post-war Marsh Report, Ottawa created a family allowance program for mothers in 1945. It was the country's first universal social program, meaning it was paid regardless of family income. Women fought to have the cheques issued in their names, not their husbands'.

In Quebec, thousands of women worked in textile mills, and Madeleine Parent was their voice. Born in 1918, Parent got her political start at McGill University where she was a student in the late 1930s. "I was a feminist during my years at college in Montreal, when it was quite clear that on the campus at McGill University, men were the predominant force and of predominant significance and women took second place."[15]

After graduating in 1941, Parent became a union organizer, first in wartime industries and then in the textile sector. She was arrested five times for labour activities and spent several months in jail. In 1944 Parent became the first woman elected to the Montreal Trades and Labour Council executive. Two years later she led a 6,000-strong strike against Dominion Textile in Quebec's cotton mills. The hundred-day strike was widely viewed as a protest against the Union Nationale government of Premier Maurice Duplessis, which was fighting union organizers with its 1937 Padlock Law.

"The conditions were really very bad … A large number of the women and children would get between 18 and 25 cents an hour," Parent recalled in a 1980 CBC interview. "The police would fire on the strikers with tear gas." It was said to have been by the order of Duplessis himself that Parent was charged with "seditious libel," a catch-all criminal charge laid against someone suspected of being communist. "They wanted to show that there was something unnatural and strange about a woman who was fighting for workers," said Parent. Although convicted, Parent was eventually acquitted. In 1969, she was instrumental in establishing the Confederation of Canadian Unions in support of an independent Canadian labour movement, free of American influence. She was also a founder of the National Action Committee on the Status of Women.

WOMEN IN POLITICS II

Under Liberal Premier Adélard Godbout, Quebec women were granted the provincial vote in 1940. "No fewer than thirteen bills dealing specifically with suffrage were needed before Quebec women could participate in choosing members of their own legislative assembly," according to Manon Tremblay in *Quebec Women and Legislative Representation*. Women were not allowed to practise law in Quebec until 1941.

In 1944, Gladys Strum was elected president of the Saskatchewan

CCF, the first woman to head a provincial political party. The following year, Strum was elected to the House of Commons as MP for the riding of Qu'Appelle. Strum was the fifth woman elected to the House of Commons and the only female MP elected in Canada's twentieth Canadian parliament. A supporter of women's rights, she said in 1945: "I submit to the House that no one has ever objected to women working. The only thing they have ever objected to is paying women for working." In 1960, Strum became the first woman elected to the Saskatchewan legislature.

After leading Quebec's early suffrage movement, Thérèse Casgrain hosted a popular Radio Canada program, *Fémina*. During the Second World War, she was one of two presidents of the Women's Surveillance Committee for the Wartime Prices and Trade Board. In a 1942 federal by-election, Casgrain ran unsuccessfully as an Independent Liberal candidate in the Charlevoix-Saguenay riding, a seat that had been held both by Casgrain's father and her husband. Casgrain then joined the Parti social démocratique du Quebec, Quebec's chapter of the CCF and became a vice-president. She was elected president of the Quebec CCF in 1951.

Following her years as a federal MP, Agnes Macphail was elected to the Ontario legislature (as a CCF member) representing East York in 1943. Macphail and Rae Luckock were the first women elected to the Ontario legislature. There, Macphail introduced the first equal pay for equal work legislation and fought to improve old-age pensions and to expand universal hospital insurance.

Following changes in 1951 to the Indian Act that permitted women to run for band election, Elsie Knott became the first woman elected as band chief. In 1952, she became leader of the 500 Mississaugas of Mudlake Indian Band, north of Peterborough.

Ellen Fairclough, a Conservative member of Parliament and her party's labour critic, introduced a private member's bill in 1955 in support of equal pay for equal work. It was the same year that the federal government ended its ban on employing married women in the civil service. Fairclough's bill was defeated. However, in 1956, following lobby efforts by the Business and Professional Women's Club, an organization Fairclough had been associated with prior to her election, the federal government passed equal pay legislation affecting seventy thousand female employees in federal jurisdictions. The bill was more symbolic than substantive, however.

In 1957, Fairclough became Canada's first female federal cabinet member when she was appointed secretary of state by Prime Minister John Diefenbaker. She was promoted to minister of citizenship and immigration in 1958. It was under her tenure as citizenship and immigration minister that status Indians were granted the right to vote federally in 1960. In 1962, Fairclough introduced regulatory changes that reduced racial discrimination in Canada's immigration policy and liberalized the country's policy on refugees.

CONSUMER RIGHTS MOVEMENT

While the federal government had welcomed women's voluntary participation in its wage and price control measures to stem wartime inflation, it did not act hospitably to consumer activism after the war. Rae Luckock was a feminist and pacifist who caused a stir as president of the Housewives and Consumers Association, the first consumer rights organization. In 1948, Luckock's association organized a historic March of a Million Names campaign, which demanded that the federal government re-institute war-era price controls in order to lower the price of consumer goods, including bread. Housewives and Consumers Association members in a hundred communities picketed stores and solicited names for petitions. Claiming 100,000 members, the association believed that consumers deserved a say in establishing prices and a say in economic policies that affected them.

The RCMP set up surveillance on the Housewives and Consumers Association in an effort to discredit its leaders as communists. Meanwhile, most male leftists didn't back the philosophical under-pinnings of the female consumers' economic agenda. Julie Guard, in *Sisters or Strangers: Immigrant, Ethnic and Racialized Women in Canada's History*, wrote: "Unlike the male-dominated left, which was primarily concerned with the relations of production, their program for social justice called for a radical renegotiation of the class relations of consumption." As suffragists had once done, consumer activists faced down their critics by leaning on women's traditional roles and responsibilities as housewives and mothers to justify their aims.

After meeting with the federal finance minister in 1947 to demand price controls, the group's reputation was undermined by news reports that some of those who had been delegates to Ottawa had ties to the Communist Party. While the women retorted that they welcomed those of all political parties, newspapers and magazines red-baited the organization and its influence waned.

CIVIL RIGHTS AND VIOLA DESMOND

By the 1940s, half of Canada's Black population, an estimated twenty thousand people, lived in Nova Scotia. The settlement of Blacks in Canada dates back to American Revolutionary War when Black United Empire Loyalists from the U.S. were given tracts of land in 1783.

Despite their long history as settlers, Black Canadians were frequently barred from hotels, restaurants, theatres and beaches in the 1940s. Segregated schools, nightclubs, churches and neighbour-hoods existed, and when they were turned away from white-owned businesses, Black patrons had little recourse. However, there were some successes. Notably in 1945, the Chateau Frontenac in Quebec was successfully sued for barring two Black Americans, a physician and his wife, from its dining room and bar.

From the 1850s to the 1950s, Black and white students "could be relegated to separate schools by law," writes Constance Backhouse in *Colour Coded: A Legal History of Racism in Canada 1900–1950.* Canadian statues allowed for schools to be set up specifically for Black children upon the request of Black parents in some jurisdictions. However, such statutes were often used to deny Black children entry into schools attended by white children. Black schools were notoriously under-funded and often lacked well-trained teachers and libraries.

Nova Scotia businesswoman Viola Desmond confronted race segregation when she challenged the owner of a segregated movie theatre on November 8, 1946. Thirty-two-year-old Desmond, owner of Vi's Studio of Beauty Culture in Halifax, was travelling on business when her car broke down in New Glasgow, N.S. Desmond operated the Desmond School of Beauty Culture, which, according to Backhouse "drew Black female students from across Nova Scotia, New Brunswick, and Quebec." In 1936, Desmond had been barred admittance at a beauty school in Halifax on the basis of her race. As a result, she studied in Montreal and New York.

Forced to spend the night in Glasgow until her car could be repaired the next day, Desmond decided to see a movie at the Roseland Theatre, *The Dark Mirror*, featuring Olivia de Havilland. At the Roseland that night, Desmond paid for a 30-cent ticket (and a 2-cent tax) and took her seat in the downstairs of the theatre. Unbeknownst to her, seats in the downstairs of the theatre cost 40 cents plus a tax of 3 cents. These seats were also considered off limits to Black moviegoers. Desmond was called back by the ticket-taker and told that "you people" were not permitted to sit downstairs. Blacks were permitted only in the upper balcony. Desmond returned to her seat on the lower level.

"I didn't realize a thing like this could happen in Nova Scotia," she said to a Canadian Press reporter, "or in any other part of Canada." The thing that occurred — after Desmond offered to pay the difference and after she explained that she had difficulty seeing the screen from the distance in the balcony — was that a police officer was summoned. He dragged her to the lobby and into a police car, and Desmond was forced to spend the night in jail.

Charged with refusing to pay a penny in tax under the province's Cinemagraphs and Amusements Act, Desmond appeared before a magistrate the next day. She was not informed she had the right to legal representation. Desmond testified that she hadn't refused to pay and, in fact, had offered to pay the extra charge. She stated that she was "being tried for being a negress and not for any felony."[16]

After being found guilty of defrauding Nova Scotia of one cent, Desmond was ordered to pay a $20 fine or spend thirty days in jail. She was also fined $6 in costs. She paid the fine and returned home. According to an article in the *Beaver* by Dean Jobb, the one-hundred-pound Desmond consulted a lawyer after seeing a doctor about the bruises incurred during her arrest. Lawyer Frederick W. Bissett took Desmond's case and the Nova Scotia Association for the Advancement of Coloured People (NSAACP) paid her legal fees.

A number of women were already fighting discrimination in Nova Scotia. The Ladies Auxiliary of the African United Baptist Association campaigned successfully to eliminate racial barriers that kept Black women out of the nursing profession. Its members included Pearleen Oliver, a founder of the NSAACP. In 1941, Oliver had led the Halifax

Coloured Citizens Improvement League's campaign to remove racially objectionable material from Nova Scotia school textbooks. Oliver urged the NSAACP to take on Desmond's case. Desmond then sued the Roseland's manager for false arrest, false imprisonment and malicious prosecution. Nova Scotia's Black newspaper, the *Clarion*, and its editor, Carrie Best, defended Desmond in print. Desmond's husband, Jack Desmond, with whom she worked side-by-side on Halifax's Gottingen Street (he was a barber), did not support her ongoing fight and the couple eventually separated.

Canada Post issued a stamp commemorating Viola Desmond's fight against segregation in Nova Scotia in 1946.

Desmond's lawyer abandoned the basis of her original complaint and appealed to the court to quash her conviction. After the case was rejected, Bissett asked the court to review the ruling, but in May 1947, the judged determined the court had no power to intervene. One of the judges, Justice William Lorimer Hall, addressed the issue of race, saying that if Desmond had appealed the ruling immediately, she may have stood a chance. "One wonders," Hall wrote, "if the manager of the theatre … was so zealous because of a bona fide belief there had been an attempt to defraud the Province of Nova Scotia of the sum of one cent, or was it a surreptitious endeavour to enforce a Jim Crow rule by misuse of a public statute." (Jim Crow is a reference to U.S. racial segregation laws.)

Although Desmond lost in court, the court of public opinion had a different verdict. In addition to the support she received from the *Clarion*, publications including *Saturday Night* magazine and the *Globe and Mail* criticized the ruling. Bissett, the white lawyer who had taken on Desmond's challenge, donated his legal fees back to organizations in support of Black civil rights. Desmond's fight led to the repeal of segregationist policies in Nova Scotia in 1954, and she was pardoned by the Nova Scotia government for her conviction posthumously in 2010.

HUMAN RIGHTS

Some Canadian jurisdictions took steps towards ending segregation and race-based policies during this time. In 1944, Ontario passed the Racial Discrimination Act, which prohibited the publication and display of any symbol, sign or notice that expressed ethnic, racial or religious discrimination. In 1947, Premier Tommy Douglas of Saskatchewan went further with the Saskatchewan Bill of Rights. It stated that "Every person in Saskatchewan irrespective of race, creed, religion, colour or ethnic or national origin shall enjoy the right … to employment … to engage in business … to own and occupy property … to enter and use public places, hotels etc. … to membership in professional and trade societies … to education and enrolment in schools and universities."

Under Canada's 1946 Citizenship Act, citizens of Canada, by birth or immigration, were no longer known as British subjects but as Canadians. Canadian women no longer lost their citizenship if they married non-Canadians. In 1947, Canada repealled the Chinese Immigration Act and Chinese Canadians were allowed to vote federally. In 1949, B.C. lifted its remaining restrictions on Chinese Canadians voting rights. The 1948 *Universal Declaration of Human*

Rights, conceived following the Holocaust during the Second World War, spurred these changes. "All human beings are born free and equal in dignity and rights," it states. Canada was an early signatory to the United Nations Convention on the Political Rights of Women in 1957, although it added a caveat stipulating that only provinces would be affected.

The Canadian Negro Women's Association, founded in 1951 by Kay Livingstone in Toronto, sought to expand opportunities for Black women. In association with other groups, the Canadian Negro Women's Association fought to end segregation in housing and employment. Nova Scotia women helped to eliminate segregated schools in 1954. Livingstone was an actor and radio host. The Canadian Women's Negro Association was the force behind the first national Black women's congress in Canada, held in 1973. Black women's congresses were then held in Montreal in 1974, in Halifax in 1976, in Windsor in 1978 and in Winnipeg in 1980. It was here that a permanent organization, the Congress of Black Women, was formed.

THE FIFTIES

An enduring myth of the 1950s era is that women aspired to become housewives, thrived in suburban comfort and eschewed paid work. Labour statistics tell a different story, however. While one third of Canadian women were employed by the end of the Second World War, nearly one quarter of women were still employed in 1951. And by the end of the 1950s, women's labour force participation rate was climbing back to the 30 percent level. Canada's population in 1951 reached fourteen million and the fertility rate of women rose slightly between 1946 and 1959, from an average of three births at the end of the Second World War to 3.5 births during the baby boom era.

The National Council of Women of Canada continued to draw

together religious women's organizations, union-affiliated women's groups, professional associations and farm women's organizations. In the 1950s, the Council's migration and citizenship committee advocated for the vote for status Indians. The Council met on a regular basis with members of the federal cabinet and during this period lobbied for a national plan of compulsory health insurance.

Due largely to lobbying by Business and Professional Women's Clubs, women were being appointed to federal boards and commissions for the first time, including those dealing with employment, fitness and vocational training and the CBC. In 1952, women were permitted to serve on juries; Manitoba was the first province to extend this right of citizenship. A federal Women's Bureau was established in 1954, and in 1955, the restriction against married women working in the federal civil service was finally removed.

The mythology of the 1950s happy housewife is derived in large part from women's magazines that fuelled a desire among women to associate personal fulfilment with consumer products. The 1950s saw the expansion of housing developments called suburbs at a time when labour saving devices, including electric washing machines, stoves and refrigerators, found new markets in a growing economy.

Women's interests continued to reach beyond the conventions of middle-class suburbia, however. The cover of the August 24, 1953, issue of *Time* magazine featured Alfred Kinsey, lead researcher of a new report on female sexuality, "Sexual Behavior in the Human Female." Kinsey's research kindled debate on undiscussed topics that included female sexual pleasure, homosexuality and fidelity. Suddenly the radical ideas of birth control advocate Margaret Sanger were given a scientific second wind.

THE WOMEN'S LIBERATION ERA, 1960–1999

I n 1960, change was in the air. Canada passed its first bill of rights, extended the federal franchise to status Indians, approved the sale of the birth control pill and witnessed the creation of a women's peace group that would steer public opinion against nuclear arms in Canada.

The debate over the next fight for women's rights was just beginning. Fernande Saint-Martin, editor of the French-language *Châtelaine*, tackled child custody and divorce, while Doris Anderson, editor of the English-language *Chatelaine* since 1957, didn't buy the happy housewife myth prevalent in women's magazines headed by men. "A lot of women used to say to me, I never read women's magazines," Anderson recalled in an interview with *Herizons* magazine in 2006. "These were very bright women at home with kids and they were climbing the walls half the time in boredom."[1]

In August 1959, *Chatelaine* broke ground with an article by Joan Finnigan titled "Should Canada Change Its Abortion Law?" It suggested that the law should be changed because illegal back alley abortions endangered women's lives. Birth control and abortion were still illegal. Then, in 1961, after a Toronto pharmacist who sold condoms was convicted and fined, Barbara Cadbury and her husband, George Cadbury, brought together fifty representatives of women's groups and protestant churches to found Planned Parenthood of Canada.[2]

No issue would galvanize women during the last four decades of the twentieth century like the issue of abortion. The birth control pill, prescribed only to married women, offered some a measure of sexual freedom; however, without the ability to terminate an unwanted

Abortion History in Canada

Source: Hennessy's Index (www.policyalternatives.ca/publications/commentary/ abortion-and-womens-rights)

 1892
Canada's first Criminal Code prohibited distribution and advertisement of contraceptives. Abortion was punishable by life imprisonment and the use or sale of contraceptives was punishable by a 2-year term in prison.

 1969
Canada decriminalized contraception and introduced a law forcing women to seek permission for abortion from a Therapeutic Abortion Committee comprised of three doctors.

 1988
In the case of Morgentaler, the Supreme Court of Canada ruled that Therapeutic Abortion Committees violated women's rights, giving women the right to terminate an unwanted pregnancy.

 1989
The Supreme Court of Canada ruled, in the case of Chantal Daigle, that "a man has no legal right to veto a woman's abortion decision."

 1995
Diane Marleau, Canada's federal health minister, deemed abortion a medically necessary procedure, forcing provinces to pay for the insured service.

pregnancy legally, women remained shackled to their reproductive capacity. An estimated 33,000 abortions were performed each year in Canada, but the practice was still illegal. Complications from abortions remained a leading cause of female hospital admissions, and, according to the Pro-Choice Canada Network, an estimated four thousand Canadian women died as a result between 1926 and 1947. Abortion-related deaths accounted for an estimated 17 to 20 percent of all maternal deaths in Canada. Women with means could travel to the U.S., where abortions were generally safer, but a majority of Canadian women seeking to terminate a pregnancy faced risky procedures. The National Council of Women, not known as a radical group, passed a motion in support of the removal of abortion from the Criminal Code at its 1971 convention.

Many reforms were achieved by sending delegations of women to lobby governments. However, diplomacy was not always first and foremost on the minds of young women in particular and besides, diplomacy had its limitations. Women's liberation was a philosophical and political movement that included but was not limited to securing women's rights. The very idea of protesting was something that women had been conditioned to regard as unfeminine. Yet in November 1961, Doris Anderson sang the praises of a group of Toronto mothers who formed a human roadblock to halt fleets of trucks that sped down their street daily and threatened their children's safety. The women had lobbied city hall to re-route traffic for two years but finally took matters into their own hands. The backlash they encountered, Anderson wrote in an editorial in *Chatelaine*, was one "that often stands in the way of women's groups when they seek a reform."

The idea of banding together was new for many women. In 1963, Betty Friedan's influential book *The Feminine Mystique* galvanized university-educated married women with its description of "the problem that had no name." The book sold a million copies and the firestorm it ignited destroyed a powerful post-war construct. "In the past sixty years we have come full circle and the American housewife is once again trapped in a squirrel cage," said one woman Friedan interviewed for the book. By the end of the decade, the myth of the happy homemaker had crashed and burned, and a political movement laying out women's modern demands arose from its ashes. Canadian literature explored similar themes of identity loss in marriage in Margaret Atwood's 1969 novel, *The Edible Woman*.

Whether they called themselves housewives, women's liberationists or new feminists, women determined to change laws, practices and beliefs that restricted women's independence and happiness. The post-war baby boom was in decline by this time and the divorce rate rose from 48 per 100,000 marriages in 1960 (a figure unchanged since 1950) to 124.3 divorces per 100,000 in 1970. Young women were living more independently than their mothers and sought increased sexual freedom. In 1960, one-quarter of university students were women. Over the next decade the proportion would climb to 37 percent.[3]

Between 1969 and 1971, women's liberation groups started in Toronto, Montreal, Regina, Winnipeg, Windsor, Ottawa, Vancouver, Kingston, Saskatoon, Guelph, Halifax, Sudbury and Thunder Bay. Some were consciousness-raising groups while others turned to political action. The first cross-Canada conference of the modern Canadian women's liberation movement took place in Saskatoon, Saskatchewan, in 1970, the same year women's studies courses were offered for the first time at the University of Toronto, McGill University, University of Waterloo, Université de Montréal and the University of Guelph. Issues once considered personal were being discussed openly by women for the first time, including sexual harassment, wife abuse, rape, abortion and sexual pleasure. Women asserted their new-found power with the slogan "the personal is political." In the end, neither the media, nor corporate institutions, nor governments, nor the legal system, nor the institution of marriage would emerge untouched. The problem that had no name now had one: sexism.

In response, feminists set out to create shelters for battered women and rape crisis centres. Some organized underground abortion services, while others formed feminist theatre groups and feminist newspapers. In Vancouver, the Women's Caucus, formed in 1968, published a feminist periodical called the *Pedestal* from 1969 to 1973. The Montreal Women's Liberation Movement was founded in 1969 and Le Front pour la libération des femmes du Québec published a feminist manifesto in 1970. A Quebec feminist periodical, *Quebecoise deboutte!*, was published from 1971 to 1975, and *Les Têtes de pioche,* which was considered more radical, published from 1976 to 1979. The *Other Woman* was Canada's first lesbian feminist newspaper when it began in Toronto in 1972, the same year *Ms. Magazine* published its first issue in New York. Meanwhile, *Kinesis* served the feminist community in Vancouver. Canadian feminist newspapers were published in the Yukon (*Optimist*), in Thunder Bay (*Northern Woman Journal,* 1973–1996) and in Halifax (*Pandora*, 1985–1994.) Specialty feminist journals included *Healthsharing, Resources for Feminist Research* and *Canadian Woman Studies*. Literary journals such as *Room of One's Own* and *Fireweed* established strong reputations.

Toronto's *Broadside* newspaper published from 1978 to 1988. *Our Lives*, Canada's first Black women's newspaper, was founded by author Dionne Brand in 1983. The *Manitoba Women's Newspaper* published its first edition in 1979 and was renamed *Herizons*. Under the direction of managing editor Deborah Holmberg Schwartz, *Herizons* was transformed from a regional publication into a national feminist magazine in September 1984. *Herizons* ceased publishing in 1987 but was re-launched in 1992 by two previous staff members (Patricia Rawson and Penni Mitchell) with the hands-on involvement of a handful of local writers, journalists, feminist educators and activists. Quebec's *La Vie en Rose* was a successful, colourful feminist magazine that published with Francine Pelletier as its editor from 1979 to 1987. It was perhaps the most successful in commercial terms, reaching a circulation of 25,000 readers. Said Pelletier, "It was as if you had embarked on a sea and the wind was carrying you," she said in *Ten Thousand Roses: The Making of a Feminist Revolution*, by Judy Rebick.[4]

More traditional women's organizations continued to push for reforms within existing institutions while women's liberationists pushed feminist philosophy in a more radical direction. As a result "extraordinarily influential groups of radical feminists denounced the major institutions of ... government and society, rejected reform through the traditional process, and opted for the building of a counterculture."[5]

Aboriginal women began to speak out against sex discrimination in the Indian Act. In 1967, Mary Two-Axe Earley started Equal Rights for Indian Women. A Mohawk from Kahnawake, Quebec, Earley had lost her Indian status after she married a New York electrical engineer. The Indian Act stripped status Indian women of their status if they married non-status men. Affected women could not live on their reserve, nor receive benefits as status Indians. Earley's campaign would take nearly twenty years to come to fruition.

In 1972, the Ontario Native Women's Association was formed to address problems relating to Aboriginal health, the effects of residential schools and addictions. The Indian Homemakers of

British Columbia and the Nova Scotia Native Women's Association addressed similar issues.

The term "second wave" is often used to classify the women's movement during this era. However, this unmenacing phrase is something of a misnomer. It was first used in 1968 by a headline writer at the *New York Times Sunday Magazine* on an article by Martha Weinman entitled, "The Second Feminist Wave." However, feminists themselves did not reference their movement as a wave. Further, the word "second" suggests there was only one previous "wave" that came before it. However, there were no less than three previous generations of women reformers in North America who accomplished important legal rights for women — in the mid-1800s, the late 1800s and the early 1900s.

QUEBEC WOMEN RISE UP

The political treatise *The Second Sex* (*Le Deuxième Sexe*), by French writer Simone de Beauvoir, conceptualized how women were viewed as "other" in patriarchal society. Originally written in French in 1949 and translated into English in 1953, Beauvoir's philosophy helped demark the philosophy behind women's modern uprising.

"One is not born, but rather becomes, a woman," de Beauvoir famously wrote. She argued that the problem of women's second-class status was that male-centred ideology had been accepted as the norm for thousands of years. That women were capable of getting pregnant, lactating and menstruating was not, de Beauvoir argued, a valid reason to relegate them to inequality as citizens. "It is when the slavery of half of humanity is abolished and with it the whole hypocritical system it implies that the 'division' of humanity will reveal its authentic meaning and the human couple will discover its true form," she wrote.

Quebec women responded to *The Second Sex* by discussing women's rights on television and in print media. In 1961, *Le Devoir* published a special section for St. Jean Baptiste Day called "A Tribute to the French-Canadian Woman." In the articles, young women were encouraged to expand their traditional roles as wives and mothers and to become more independent. Women expressed a desire for equality and greater liberties. Thérèse Casgrain and broadcaster Jeanne Sauvé were among those leading the feminist charges in Quebec. Sauvé was later a cabinet minister in the Trudeau government. Casgrain, who ran nine times for public office and championed women's rights for fifty years, was appointed to the Senate in 1970.

Quebec's women's movement influenced and was influenced by Quebec's Quiet Revolution, a period in which social change was swift and sweeping. Culturally, economically and politically, the values of Quebeckers underwent a radical transformation. The state took over many public services that were once controlled by the church. Women took on less traditional roles during this time, and labour unions made headway, while the influence of the Catholic Church shrank. Quebec women's birth rate fell by 50 percent between 1959 and 1969.

In 1963, pressure from women's organizations prompted the Quebec government to set up a commission to examine women's legal status within the province's Civil Code. Claire Kirkland-Casgrain, who in 1961 had been the first woman to be elected to the Quebec national assembly, was instrumental to the commission. A lawyer and later a judge, Kirkland Casgrain was an activist with the Fédération des femme libérales du Quebec. She recalled being "revolted" when she learned of married women's legal status under Quebec's Civil Code. The 1964 reforms finally gave married women in Quebec full legal capacity, enabling them to sign contracts and exercise control over their property. In 1966, a new umbrella group, the Fédération des femmes du Québec, was formed by Thérèse Casgrain, and others; notably it had no religious ties. For many Quebecoise, the desire to be "Maîtres chez nous!" ("Masters in our own house," the slogan of the Quiet Revolution) had a gendered parallel. The Front de libération des femmes declared in 1969 that there would be no women's liberation without the liberation of Quebec and no Quebec liberation without the liberation of women.

THE VOICE OF WOMEN

Galvanized by opposition to the global nuclear arms buildup, the Voice of Women (VOW), founded in July 1960, became one of the most successful women's organizations in Canada.

An impetus for the Voice of Women was the 1958 formation of the North American Air Defense agreement (NORAD). Canada and the U.S. established NORAD as a response to Soviet long-range nuclear bombers. NORAD would, in theory, provide aerial defence of North America in the event of a nuclear attack from the Soviet Union. It was at this time, during the height of the Cold War, that Canada agreed to deploy fifty-six Bomarc missiles from the U.S. in North Bay, Ontario, and La Macaza, Quebec. When it was discovered that the missiles would be fitted with nuclear warheads, a public debate known as the Bomarc Missile Crisis ensued.

In response, *Toronto Star* columnist Lotta Dempsey wrote an article in May 1960 calling on women to weigh in, and a public meeting organized by Helen Tucker, Josephine Davis, Dorothy Henderson and Beth Touzel saw the formation of the Voice of Women. The new organization aimed to ban nuclear weapons from Canada's waters, airspace and soil, and keep radioactive waste out of the country. In November 1960, the newly formed Halifax chapter of the VOW met in Muriel Duckworth's living room and the twenty-three women present decided to protest the dumping of nuclear waste by a U.S. company 150 miles off the coast of Yarmouth, N.S. Media coverage helped publicize the issue and Canada eventually blocked the dumping.[6]

The VOW also condemned Canada's involvement in testing chemical and biological warfare agents and encouraged Ottawa not to back the U.S. during the Cuban Missile Crisis. The organization was credited by Howard Green, Canada's external affairs minister during the Cuban Missile Crisis, with delaying Canada's decision to place its air force on the same NORAD alert as the U.S.[7]

An important aim of the organization was to work with anti-nuclear activists internationally to rid the world of nuclear arms. The five thousand members of the VOW were not only opposed to war, but appealed to national leaders to alleviate the causes of war. They adhered to the VOW's aim to work for "the economic and social betterment of mankind and to provide a means for women to exercise responsibility for the family of mankind."

The VOW purposely and strategically linked women's protective roles as mothers to their opposition to nuclear arms. They promoted a national campaign that measured levels of strontium-90, a dangerous by-product of exposure to nuclear fallout from U.S. bomb tests, in Canadian children's baby teeth. In 1962, the VOW initiated an international women's conference which brought women from the Soviet Union and other socialist countries. The group campaigned in favour of an international treaty that resulted in a partial nuclear test ban in 1963. Under Prime Minister Pierre Trudeau, Canada signed the Nuclear Non-Proliferation Treaty, which took force in 1970.

Muriel Duckworth served as president of the VOW from 1967 to 1971. Duckworth had been involved in the League for Social Reconstruction, one of the many organizations that came together after the Second World War to form the CCF. For more than thirty

Women protest the presence of nuclear arms in Canada at an Ottawa protest on September 25, 1961.
Photo: Duncan Cameron, Library and Archives Canada.

years, Duckworth worked on international peace issues and the VOW was instrumental in mobilizing Canadian public opinion in favour of nuclear arms control. It fought the deployment of cruise and Pershing missiles in Canada and popularized the idea of nuclear-free zones.

Civil disobedience was a natural strategy for peace activists. One of the VOW's first presidents, Kay MacPherson, was jailed after trying to present a statement to the secretary general of NATO during a 1964 conference in Paris. MacPherson and others were protesting a proposal for a multilateral force that would have allowed NATO naval commanders to launch a nuclear strike.

Though the VOW did not describe itself as a feminist organization when it started, its leading members were active feminists. Thérèse Casgrain, long-time feminist crusader, carried the VOW banner in Quebec. Kay MacPherson went on to become president of the

National Action Committee on the Status of Women in 1977. Most anti-nuclear supporters were women. According to a 1983 Gallup poll, 57 percent of women were against cruise missile testing in Canada, compared to 39 percent of men.

In Canada, pacifism informed the philosophy of the women's liberation movement in large part due to the VOW. In 1978, the VOW participated in the historic U.N. Special Session on Disarmament that outlined a plan for global nuclear arms reduction. In the 1980s, the VOW protested the flights of low-level NATO jets over Innu communities in Labrador.

THE CIVIL RIGHTS INFLUENCE

The civil rights movement had a direct impact on the women's liberation movement in North America. Many organizers of public protests that led to the 1964 passage of the U.S. Civil Rights Act — including the Montgomery, Alabama, bus boycott and the Freedom Rides that saw students beaten and buses burned — were women. Female riders were among those jailed and assaulted. Women also instigated four court cases in the U.S. and Canada that challenged segregated seating policies. The first was Ida B. Wells, a teacher who refused when a train conductor ordered her to give up her seat. In 1944, Irene Morgan, a factory worker recovering from a miscarriage, refused to give up her seat on a Greyhound bus and when a sheriff's deputy gave her an arrest warrant, she tore it up and kicked him in the groin. Next was Canadian beautician Viola Desmond, who went to court to fight segregated seating in a New Glasgow, Nova Scotia, theatre (see Chapter 7). Rosa Parks, the most famous of the seat challengers, was the fourth. A veteran activist with the National Association for the Advancement of Coloured People (NAACP), Parks refused a white rider's request to relinquish her seat on a bus in 1955. Black bus riders in Montgomery, Alabama, successfully boycotted bus companies in a campaign driven by women.

Anna Holmes, columnist at the *Washington Post*, wrote in 2011, "the story of institutional racism, segregation and overt or perceived threats of violence — and the efforts to combat them — is, in many ways, the story of women. And their efforts, directly and indirectly, paved the way for the modern feminist movement."[8]

In Canada, the civil rights movement on the west coast was where Rosemary Brown got her activist start with the B.C.

In 1972, Rosemary Brown was the first Black woman elected to a Canadian legislature, in B.C.
Barbara Woodley, Labatt Breweries of Canada, Library and Archives Canada, 1993-234, PA-186871.

Association for the Advancement of Coloured People in 1956. The organization campaigned for legislative and educational reforms, including anti-discrimination measures (called civil rights in the U.S.) and actively opposed segregation practices in Canada.

Brown, who was born in Jamaica, experienced discrimination as a Black immigrant and as a Canadian woman. In her autobiography, *Being Brown: A Very Public Life*, Brown recalled that, "to be Black and female in a society which is both racist and sexist is to be in the unique position of having nowhere to go but up." Brown spoke candidly about how Betty Friedan's 1963 book, *The Feminine Mystique,* transformed her depression into a political force: "Suddenly it was all there, the story of my life … The fact that I was not alone reassured me and mobilized me."

A founding member of the Vancouver Status of Women Council,

Brown became the first Black woman elected to a provincial legislature in 1972 when she sat in the B.C legislature. She held the seat for sixteen years. In 1975, Brown ran for the leadership of the federal NDP and became the first woman to contest the leadership of a major national political party in Canada. Her slogan was "Brown Is Beautiful." Brown lost on the fourth ballot to Ed Broadbent, who had 984 votes to Brown's 658. After leaving politics in 1988, Brown headed MATCH International, a Canadian international women's development agency. She was later chief commissioner of the Ontario Human Rights Commission from 1993 to 1996.

In the U.S., the Presidential Commission on the Status of Women had been set up by U.S. President John F. Kennedy in 1961. It was the price that former First Lady Eleanor Roosevelt extracted from Kennedy in exchange for her support of his 1960 presidential bid. Eleanor Roosevelt had been instrumental in the creation of the United Nations' *Universal Declaration on Human Rights* in 1948, which encouraged member states to promote "universal respect for, and observance of, human rights and fundamental freedoms for all without distinction as to race, sex, language, or religion." She chaired the U.S. Presidential Commission on the Status of Women until her death in 1962. Following the lead of their American sisters, Canadian women sought a commission of their own.

The mobilization of students politicized many during this era. In Montreal, a riot ensued at Sir George Williams University (now part of Concordia University) after students of an assistant biology professor reported that the professor routinely failed many of his Black students. A committee was struck to investigate, but two Black professors on the committee quit, stating that the committee was not impartial. In February 1969, students occupied the university and demanded the dismissal of the professor. When police arrived to remove the demonstrators, tables, chairs and computers were thrown out the windows and down the escalators. Thirty women and sixty men were arrested. One of them was Anne Cools, a twenty-seven-year-old Barbados-born student found guilty of willfully obstructing the use of the computer centre. The professor was never fired, yet the riot "awakened the Black Power movement in Canada," according to Dionne Brand in her 1994 book, *Bread Out of Stone*. In 1983, Cools became Canada's first Black senator.

THE ROYAL COMMISSION

Canadian women, among them federal Secretary of State Judy LaMarsh, pushed for a women's commission. When first approached about the idea, however, Prime Minister Lester B. Pearson "backed off as if stung with nettle," as LaMarsh recalled in her biography, *Memoirs of a Bird in a Gilded Cage*. Pearson apparently feared that such a commission could tread upon the jurisdiction of the provinces. "It seemed odd that in some men's minds women belong predominantly to the provinces," LaMarsh wryly observed. There was no question that "an airing of women's complaints in a national forum" was needed, LaMarsh wrote. Frustrated by her treatment as an anomaly by the media since her election, LaMarsh grew tired of her unofficial role as "woman's watchdog."

However, Laura Sabia, president of the Canadian Federation of University Women, and Quebec's Thérèse Casgrain were happy to take on the job of woman's watchdog. Sabia brought together English women's organizations in 1966 to form the Committee on Equality for Women (CEW), an organization that called for a royal commission. The fifty women who attended the committee's first meeting represented thirty-two organizations, including the YWCA, the WCTU, the VOW, the Imperial Order Daughters of the Empire, the

Canadian Federation of Business and Professional Women's Clubs, the National Council of Jewish Women, the National Council of Women of Canada and the Federated Women's Institutes.

Under Sabia's leadership, representatives of the CEW and high-profile French feminists Thérèse Casgrain and Rejane Laberge-Colas, the Fédération des femmes du Quebec's president, met with Pearson. As N.E.S. Griffiths wrote in *The Splendid Vision: Centennial History of the National Council of Women 1893–1993*, "the presence of French-Canadian women as delegates to the Prime Minister requesting the establishment of the Royal Commission was of crucial importance."

On February 3, 1967, after Sabia threatened to summons a two-million-strong women's march in Ottawa to shame government into action, a commission on women, to be chaired by CBC broadcaster Florence Bird, was announced. The Royal Commission on the Status of Women set out to recommend steps the federal government could take to ensure equal opportunities and improve the status of women in all aspects of Canadian society, particularly with reference to federal statutes, regulations and policies that concerned the rights of women. The six commissioners, four women and two men, included farm activist Lola M. Lange; Jeanne Lapointe, a literature professor; aeronautical engineer Elsie Gregory MacGill; Doris Ogilvie, a New Brunswick judge; demography professor Jacques Henripin; and John Humphrey, a McGill law professor who had helped to craft the *Universal Declaration of Human Rights* while representing Canada on the United Nations Human Rights Commission.

In 1968, the commission's public hearings began in fourteen cities, and over the next ten months they attracted strong public interest. The commission received 468 briefs and heard additional testimony out of the public spotlight. All of this attested to widespread problems experienced by women in all walks of life. The commission resulted in increased public awareness of the prevalence of sex discrimination, which bolstered women's demands for change. It altered the political landscape in Canada and furthered the idea that government had a responsibility to ensure that its laws, employment practices and regulations were not discriminatory. The expectation that governments should act to advance women's participation in society entered into the public realm during an era when social welfare in Canada was expanding. Social inequities were commonly addressed through government programs. By the mid-1960s, Canadians had publicly paid hospital care, an unemployment insurance program, a pension plan and a mother's allowance.

Many equality measures did not involve public spending — for example, divorce liberalization. In 1968, Justice Minister Pierre Trudeau sought to simplify Canada's divorce laws, and the result was that marital breakdown became the sole grounds for divorce. Trudeau also introduced an omnibus bill (1968–1969) to amend the Criminal Code to legalize birth control, decriminalize abortion under some circumstances and decriminalize homosexual acts. Trudeau defended his controversial bill stating, "There's no place for the state in the bedrooms of the nation."

Trudeau became prime minister in 1968. However, in spite of his liberal views on divorce, he was not widely considered to be a strong supporter of women's causes. Nonetheless, it fell to Trudeau to usher in the royal commission report in 1970, a detail that bestowed him with a reputation as a supporter of women's rights.

In November 1970, the Royal Commission's final report was released. The document listed 167 women's grievances in the form of recommendations. The implementation of those recommendations and the growth of the political movement behind them would form the core agenda of the Canadian women's movement until the end of the century.

The report drew attention to the need for safe and legal abortion. It said that equal pay laws should be applied and it called for affirmative action for employers in federal jurisdictions. The report recommended ways to eliminate "occupation sex-typing" and eschewed discrimination based on marital status in hiring and advancement. The Royal Commission called on government to take active steps to achieve equality in education for girls and to improve "family life" education. A section on law reform called for a shorter time of separation (one year instead of three years) as a requirement for divorce, as well as an end to the stipulation that victims of rape must be "of previously chaste character" before an accused could be convicted.

The report called on government to end sex discrimination in the Canada Pension Plan and the Quebec Pension Plan. It championed ending discrimination in the Indian Act, specifically the stipulation that status Indian women who married non-Indians lost their Indian status. The report called for paid maternity leave within the unemployment insurance program, advanced publicly paid daycare and recommended an end to discrimination against single mothers. It called for parity for women in the appointment of senators as well as for the creation of alcoholism treatment programs for women. Seven recommendations were devoted to discrimination in the Immigration Act and eight addressed measures needed to improve the treatment of female offenders within the justice system, including "flexible and imaginative programs, in particular the cottage-type 'open' system of detention."

Upon the release of the report, the breadth of its intended reforms was captured by *Toronto Star* reporter Anthony Westell: "This 488-page book, in its discreet green, white and blue cover, demands radical change ... between man and woman. The history of the problem it describes and seeks to solve is not 100 years of Confederation, but the story of mankind."[9]

To ensure the Royal Commission's recommendations were acted on, women transformed the CEW into the National Ad Hoc Committee on the Status of Women in 1971. It would be an umbrella group, similar to the Fédération des femmes du Québec and the National Women's Council of Canada. In 1972, the words "ad hoc" were dropped from the name. The National Action Committee on the Status of Women (NAC) expanded over the next two decades to include a membership of more than 600 organizations. Laura Sabia was its first president in 1972 and NAC went on to serve as an influential national feminist umbrella organization for the next thirty years.

NAC, and its member organizations, lobbied governments to enact the Royal Commission's recommendations, and to act upon new women's issued identified as priorities at NAC conferences, which attracted as many as five hundred delegates. Following its annual conferences, volunteers met with federal politicians to present their recommendations. Provincial action committees also started to address regional concerns and to push provinces to implement policies in the spirit of the Royal Commission.

Lorna Marsden, who had attended the founding meeting of NAC in April 1972 was president of NAC from 1975 to 1977. Prime Minister Pierre Trudeau appointed Marsden to the Senate in 1984 and she served until 1992 when she resigned to take an academic position.

In 1973, Ottawa created the Canadian Advisory Council on the Status of Women (CACSW) to advise the federal government on equality issues affecting women. Provincial governments created similar councils. Made up of political appointees, these councils provided advice to status of women ministers on how to advance women's equality efforts. Advisory councils differed from activist organizations, which were made up of grassroots feminists — that is, membership-based voluntary organizations that lobbied governments and agencies and maintained a strong public presence through in the media. Ottawa established a federal branch called Status of Women Canada in 1976 to promote gender equality and to ensure the full participation of women in the economic, social, cultural and political life of the country. An equality funding arm, the Secretary of State Women's Program, was set up in 1973 to support to women's equality organizations. It supported research projects involving a multitude of women's issues and backed a host of initiatives designed to improve the status of women. In 1986, the program dispersed $12,400,000.[10]

Dozens of new women's organizations formed. The Native Women's Association of Canada started in 1974, the National Association of Women and the Law was created in 1975, and l'Association des femmes collaboratrices began in 1976. The Lesbian Mothers Defence Fund of Toronto, founded in 1979, supported lesbian mothers facing custody disputes, according to Francie Wyland, writing in the journal *Resources for Feminist Research* in March 1983. Other organizations on the national scene included the Canadian Research Institute for the Advancement of Women, the Canadian Congress for Learning Opportunities for Women, the Canadian Day Care Advocacy Group, la Fédération nationale des femmes canadiennes-françaises, the National Organization of Immigrant and Visible Minority Women of Canada, Media Watch and the Canadian Association of Sexual Assault Centres. The Feminist Party of Canada was started by Moira Armour in 1979 to increase the participation of women in electoral politics.

NAC enjoyed a high profile and, in 1984, its president, Chaviva

Hosek, orchestrated a nationally televised political leaders' debate on women's issues during the federal election. Following the 1984 election, twenty-seven women were elected to the House of Commons, representing nearly 10 percent of Canada's MPs.

As a result of reforms backed by the Royal Commission, the waiting period for divorce was reduced from three years to one year. Changes in public and private pension plans were made during this time. Other changes recommended by the commission, such as improvements to women's prison conditions, would have to wait until the end of the century. A federally sponsored commission of inquiry into Canada's federal prison for women in Kingston, Ontario, noted, "The prison is an old fashioned, dysfunctional labyrinth of claustrophobic and inadequate spaces holding 142 prisoners ... It has been described as 'unfit for bears.'"[11]

A new organization for women with disabilities, the DisAbled Women's Network Canada (DAWN), started following a 1985 conference. DAWN was formed to confront forms of discrimination that affect disabled women on the basis of gender and ability. DAWN successfully demonstrated that notions of "ability" and "normal" are socially constructed ideas that reinforce a dominant culture that is able-bodied and male-dominated. The organization was set up with a view to end the poverty, isolation, discrimination and violence experienced by women with disabilities and to fight for women with disabilities to have freedom of choice in all aspects of their lives.

The federal Divorce Act was amended to include new child support guidelines in 1997, which helped to standardize levels of child support. The guidelines tied child support levels to the income of the payer (usually the father) and the number of children. The guidelines came in response to a Supreme Court ruling that child support was to be taxable in the hands of the payer, not the recipient.[12]

In the 1990s, NAC underwent a political shift. Ostensibly, the shift was to make the organization more inclusive of "grassroots" women, that is, women not affiliated with established political parties. Since its inception, NAC presidents tended to be women with ties to the Liberal, Conservative or New Democratic parties, although the organization did not endorse political parties or candidates. During the 1988 federal election, NAC joined a national coalition of unions, women's groups and others who opposed the proposed North American Free Trade Agreement (NAFTA). The issue was a divisive one, and the Liberals vowed to renegotiate NAFTA during the election, but supported the agreement following the election of Progressive Conservative Prime Minister Brian Mulroney in 1988. The organization had begun a shift away from partisan politics towards coalition efforts.[13]

Then, under Judy Rebick's leadership in 1992, NAC backed the "No" side in the Charlottetown Accord, a constitutional reform package endorsed by the Liberals, Conservatives and NDP. It would have amended the Canadian Constitution to decentralize many federal powers, recognize Quebec as a distinct society and seek Quebec's consent to the Constitution Act of 1982. Many women feared that a decentralized government would weaken social programs, and NAC believed that the Accord created a hierarchy of rights in which women ranked behind linguistic minorities, Aboriginals and Quebeckers. Said Rebick: "A lot of women activists at the grassroots level were saying No. Women of colour were strongly for the No. The Aboriginal women at the executive told us their communities were strongly for the No. And so were the trade union women."[14] Although there was a risk that NAC's position could strain its relations with federal political parties, it believed opposing the Accord was in the best interests of women. Pierre Trudeau and other prominent Canadians also opposed the Accord, and it failed in a referendum.

The first woman of colour to be elected president of NAC was Sunera Thobani in 1993. During Thobani's tenure, NAC focused on economic issues; it co-sponsored a successful March against Poverty in Quebec and addressed the negative impact of neoliberal policies on women. Though NAC was officially non-partisan, Thobani said during the 1993 federal election of the Conservative platform, "The cuts to social programs — we're going to see this society transformed in a fundamental and radical manner and what we want to do at this point is to try to stop them going further along that path."[15]

WOMEN IN FEDERAL POLITICS

After winning a by-election in 1960 at age thirty-four, Judy LaMarsh quickly gained a reputation as an outspoken MP. According to an *Ottawa Citizen* article, LaMarsh was known for "a caustic turn of wit and sharp mind." In 1963, she was appointed minister of health and welfare in the Liberal administration of Prime Minister Lester B. Pearson. During this time, the legislative groundwork for medicare was laid by her department. Under her ministry, the Canada Pension Plan was introduced in 1965. LaMarsh was then appointed secretary of state, a position that saw her introduce Canada's Broadcasting Act and preside over Canada's 1967 Centennial celebrations. In 1969, Canada's female editors voted LaMarsh the most influential woman of the decade.

In 1972, five women, including the first three female Quebec MPs, were elected to the House of Commons. One of them, Monique Bégin, had been executive secretary to the Royal Commission on the Status of Women. She was appointed minister of national revenue in the Trudeau administration. Bégin became Canada's minister of health and welfare in 1977 and later introduced the Canada Health

Act in 1984. Another newly elected woman from Quebec, Jeanne Sauvé, was appointed minister of state for science and technology in 1972. She later served as minister of the environment in 1974 and as minister of communications in 1975. In 1980, Sauvé became Canada's first woman speaker in the House of Commons and in 1984 she was Canada's first female governor general.

Flora MacDonald, also first elected in 1972, made national headlines when she defied the unwritten dress code for female Parliamentarians and wore a pantsuit into the House of Commons. Later, in 1979, MacDonald became Canada's first female secretary of state for external affairs. A red Tory, MacDonald ran unsuccessfully for the leadership of the Progressive Conservative party in 1976, losing to Joe Clark. She also served as minister of employment and immigration and minister of communications.

Grace MacInnes, a CCF MP elected in 1965, pressed government on issues stemming from the Royal Commission, including birth control and abortion, until her retirement in 1974. The daughter of former Winnipeg North Centre MP J.S. Woodsworth (1921–1942), MacInnes was the only female MP in the House of Commons in 1970 when a group of women staged a sit-in in the speakers' gallery to protest Canada's abortion law.

Judy Erola became the first female minister responsible for the status of women, in 1981, during the Trudeau administration. Previously, four men had held the portfolio. Erola served as minister of state for mines, minister of state for social development and minister of consumer and corporate affairs. Erola was also the first woman appointed to the federal government's cabinet priorities and planning committee, an inner group that determines the direction of government policy.

In the 1980 federal election, only fourteen women had been

elected to the House of Commons, making up 5 percent of MPs. After the 1984 federal election, female MPs reached the 10 percent mark in the Tory landslide in which nineteen of the twenty-nine women elected were Progressive Conservatives. The highest profile female Progressive Conservative MPs were Flora McDonald, Pat Carney and Barbara McDougall. Carney was appointed to cabinet as minister of energy, mines and resources where she dismantled the National Energy Program. In 1986, she became minister of international trade and was a key player in negotiating the North America Free Trade Agreement. She was later appointed to the Senate. Barbara McDougall served as minister responsible for the status of women from 1986 to 1990, as well as employment and immigration minister.

Of the five women Liberals elected in 1984, Sheila Copps was the most outspoken. Copps served as minister of the environment and minister of Canadian heritage and was an advocate for women entering politics. She frequently traded barbs with Conservative MP John Crosbie. In 1985, he told Copps to "Quiet down, baby" in the House of Commons, to which Copps bluntly replied, "I'm not his baby and I'm nobody's baby." In 1987 Copps was the first MP to have a baby while in office. An unapologetic feminist, Copps was the target of sexist remarks in the House. Tory MP Bill Kempling called her a "slut" while Reform MP Ian McClelland landed in hot water for referring to her as a "bitch." She ran unsuccessfully for the leadership of the Liberal Party in 1990. In 1993, Copps became Canada's first woman deputy prime minister, under Prime Minister Jean Chrétien.

In 1988, Ethel Blondin-Andrew became the first Aboriginal woman elected to the House of Commons. As described by Caroline Andrew and Manon Tremblay, editors of *Women and Political Representation in Canada*, Aboriginal women and women of colour "face numerous barriers to enhanced political participation and representation based on social class and gender. The underrepresentation of women from ethnic and racialized minorities results from a complex set of factors that also includes ethnic ranking and prejudice, racism as well as fluency in official languages, immigrant status and other factors."[16]

In 1988, Audrey McLachlan, an NDP MP representing the Yukon, became the first woman to lead a major political party after the resignation of NDP leader Ed Broadbent. McLaughlin, a social worker, was also a feminist. Although her party did not oppose NAFTA, she argued going into the 1993 federal election that "the economic policies of deregulation, disastrous trade deals, privatization, and high interest rates to control inflation haven't worked ... That's the fundamental problem."[17]

In 1993, Jean Augustine, an Ontario Liberal, became the first Black woman elected to the House of Commons. Augustine served as the parliamentary secretary to Prime Minister Jean Chrétien from 1994 to 1996, and was the minister of state for multiculturalism.

Following the resignation of Brian Mulroney as leader of the Progressive Conservative Party in 1993, the party elected Kim Campbell as its leader. First elected in 1988 to represent the riding of Vancouver Centre, Campbell spent five years as a cabinet minister in the Mulroney government. She served as minister of Indian affairs, minister of justice and minister of defence. Campbell was also instrumental in reconfiguring Canada's rape shield law after it was struck down as unconstitutional. Under her leadership, Bill C-49 was passed and the questioning of a rape victim about her sexual history in court became much more difficult in Canada.[18]

At a women's media conference in November 1992, Campbell spoke candidly about the sexism she encountered as a female politician. For example, she referenced a *Toronto Star* article in which she was characterized as "crushingly ambitious." "What is crushingly ambitious?" Campbell rhetorically asked the 450 journalists, calling the term a put-down. "We cannot encourage women to participate and then punish them for the effrontery of trying to do more," she said.

After Campbell was sworn in as prime minister on June 13, 1993, she called an election, after which she went down to defeat. Her reign as Canada's first female prime minister was a mere 132 days. During the

Kim Campbell became the first female prime minister of Canada in 1993 when she was elected leader of the Progressive Conservative Party.
Photo: kimcampbell.com.

campaign, she "faced criticism in the media and from her opponents for everything from her weight and twice-divorced marital status, to her supposed lack of political experience. Her predecessor, Brian Mulroney, had not held public office before becoming party leader."[19]

Campbell identified herself as a feminist, yet she was a controversial figure who did not automatically gain the support of the feminist movement. NAC President Sunera Thobani said of Campbell in the lead up to her election in 1993, "Just because we have a woman prime minister doesn't mean that women in Canada have achieved equality. We have to look at the policies that they put forward and what they are going to do."[20]

Political science professor Manon Tremblay noted that, in the 1993 federal election, women were more likely than men to have voted for the two parties then led by women. "In 1997, women were less inclined than men to vote for the Reform Party and more inclined to vote for the New Democratic Party."[21] Research shows that women

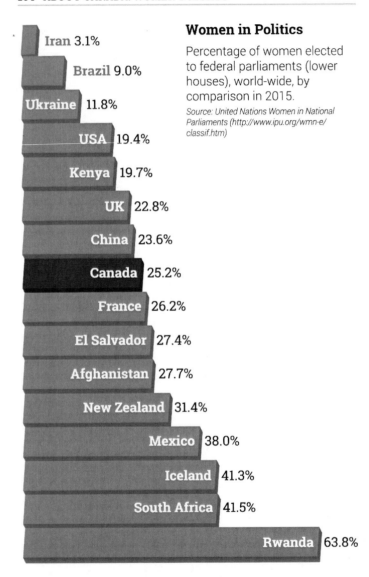

Women in Politics

Percentage of women elected to federal parliaments (lower houses), world-wide, by comparison in 2015.

Source: United Nations Women in National Parliaments (http://www.ipu.org/wmn-e/classif.htm)

Iran 3.1%

Brazil 9.0%

Ukraine 11.8%

USA 19.4%

Kenya 19.7%

UK 22.8%

China 23.6%

Canada 25.2%

France 26.2%

El Salvador 27.4%

Afghanistan 27.7%

New Zealand 31.4%

Mexico 38.0%

Iceland 41.3%

South Africa 41.5%

Rwanda 63.8%

are more supportive of programs that strengthen public programs compared to male voters.

When Audrey McLachlan stepped down as leader in 1995, she was replaced by Alexa McDonough, who had been involved in Nova Scotia politics since 1980. McDonough was first elected to Parliament in 1997 representing Halifax. In that election, McDonough led a resurgence of the party that saw the NDP win 21 seats across Canada. Importantly, the party regained its official party status in the House of Commons. In the next federal election, the NDP won thirteen seats and McDonough oversaw a process of party renewal for the NDP.

DISCRIMINATION AT WORK

Throughout this era, women fought to end discriminatory employment practices. Stewardesses (now called flight attendants) were routinely fired when they married or turned thirty-two years of age — whichever came first. It wasn't until 1978 that they won the right to work after thirty-two and after marriage.

Female workers made up 28.8 percent of the paid workforce in 1964, a proportion that grew to 39.9 percent by 1971. Approximately half of female workers at this time were married. In 1969, equal pay provisions had been added to the B.C. Human Rights Act, Nova Scotia's Equal Pay Act and Saskatchewan's Labour Standards Act. The number of women in unions increased during this time as public services and programs expanded. However, most collective agreements stipulated different wage rates for male and female workers. The first women's committees within unions were struck in this era to address women's concerns. In 1975, Grace Hartman became the first female president of the Canadian Union of Public Employees, Canada's largest union. A trailblazing union organizer for thirty years, Hartman fought for pay equity, fair pay and peace.

Thanks to women's efforts, the Canada Labour (Standards) Code was amended in 1971 to provide equal pay for equivalent work for federal employees; it also provided for maternity leave of seventeen weeks for qualifying workers. Federal and provincial governments established women's bureaus to advance women's training and employment opportunities and develop measures to end sex discrimination at work. In 1972 the Office of Equal Opportunities for Women was established within the federal Public Service Commission and the Women's Bureau was created in the federal Department of Labour.

The War Veterans Allowance Act was amended to include female veterans. In 1971, the Canadian Forces began to include women on the same basis as men in all job classifications except combat arms, sea-going duties and isolated positions. It was in 1987 that the Canadian Forces accepted women in combat roles. The RCMP admitted its first female recruits in 1974.

The Canadian Human Rights Act, enacted in 1975, established a Human Rights Commission to hear employment complaints based on a list of grounds of discrimination, including sex and marital status, for employees in federally regulated workplaces. Quebec's 1975 Charter of Human Rights and Freedoms outlined human rights irrespective of sex, colour, race and disability. Discrimination based on sexual orientation in Quebec was prohibited in 1977, making Quebec the first province to do so.

By 1983, the Canadian Human Rights Act had been amended to prohibit sexual harassment in workplaces under federal jurisdiction. However, more was needed to advance women at work and the federal government struck a one-woman Royal Commission on Equality in Employment in 1984. Its chairwoman, Rosalie Abella, an Ontario judge, backed away from the use of the term "affirmative action" in her report; the term had been negatively associated with quotas in the

U.S. Instead, Abella coined the term "employment equity." The Abella Commission report, which made 117 recommendations, advocated for goals and targets instead of quotas and firmly defended the need for enforcement. Federal employment minister Flora MacDonald introduced employment equity legislation for the federal civil service in 1985; however, most women's and disability groups believed MacDonald's law was weak and lacked accountability. Twenty-five years later, women would make up 54.7 percent of the federal workforce, Aboriginal people would make up 4.5 percent, people with disabilities made up 5.9 percent, and 9.8 percent of the federal civil service would be made up of people categorized as visible minorities.

The need for remedial action was underscored by the fact that in 1985, the average woman who worked full-time in Canada earned just 64.9 percent of the average man's full-time salary. In the 1980s, many jurisdictions implemented affirmative action programs within their civil services to advance the hiring of women, Aboriginal people, people with disabilities and members of visible minority groups.

Starting in 1985, pay equity, or equal pay for work of equal value, was legislated in the public sector in Manitoba, Nova Scotia, New Brunswick and PEI. In Quebec and Ontario, both public and some private sectors were subject to pay equity laws. Pay equity was developed as a process to evaluate and compare the value of work done by employees in male-dominated and female-dominated classes of work. Pay equity adjustments were phased in for affected work classifications over a period of time with the involvement of affected unions. It is estimated that pay equity wage adjustments closed the wage gap by approximately 5 percent. Pay discrimination on the basis of sex and marital status were prohibited during this time by human rights legislation. Equal pay also became a requirement of employment standards legislation in most provinces and jurisdictions.

In 1986, the federal government passed its pay equity act. In the years that followed, the Public Service Alliance of Canada negotiated to have 230,000 current and former public service employees receive pay equity adjustments that were then ordered by the courts. After appealing these decisions for years, the federal government finally came to an agreement worth $3.5 billion in pay equity adjustments.

Publicly funded daycare was identified as essential to furthering women's labour force participation in the final report of the Royal Commission on the Status of Women. "The time is past," it observed, "when society can refuse to provide community child care services in the hope of dissuading mothers from leaving their children and going to work."

Indeed, in the final two decades of the twentieth century, a national system of affordable, accessible, quality childcare remained high on the feminist agenda. In 1984, Conservative Prime Minister Brian Mulroney promised to create a national daycare program, but he failed to advance a plan that secured the backing of daycare advocates. They wanted a program that would ensure affordability, accessibility and quality, including national standards. The federal government undertook a Task Force on Child Care chaired by Katie Cook, a former president of the Canadian Advisory Council of the Status of Women. It issued a 380-page report in March 1986. The task force held hearings and consulted experts; its final report outlined funding options and estimated costs for a national daycare program, including options for expanded parental leave. According to the *Report of the Task Force on Child Care,* "121,000 working mothers were forced to leave or refuse a job offer because they could not find adequate child care arrangements."[22]

However, the demand for a national daycare program continued to be ignored by both Liberal and Conservative administrations and responsibility for public daycare fell to the provinces and territories. By 1999, there were 397,970 licensed childcare spaces in Canada, according to Statistics Canada, compared to just 16,791 in 1971. In 1997, Quebec began to phase in a province-wide system of licensed child care that would support close to 200,000 child-care spaces at a cost to parents of just $5 a day.

Another approach to the care of children involved the hiring of foreign domestic workers. Under the 1981 foreign domestic movement program, foreign domestic workers were required to follow strict rules, including the stipulation that they live with their employers. No other class of foreign workers was required to live with an employer. Under the 1992 live-in caregiver program, the training requirements women needed in order to apply were increased.

Meanwhile, a new immigration act was passed in 1976 that removed some forms of discrimination. For example the immigration term "head of family," which had been interpreted as "husband," was replaced with wording that could reference a male or female applicant. Notwithstanding this change, sponsored immigrant and refugee women and domestic workers remained especially vulnerable to abusive relationships because of their lack of autonomy and independence.

Until the late 1980s, Canada's Immigration and Refugee Board did not consider the impact of gender. For example, an Immigrant and Refugee Board judge ruled against admitting a woman from China after the judge determined that China's one-child policy, which required women to abort further pregnancies, was not a matter of persecution for women but a matter of "economic logic." After this, Citizenship and Immigration Canada established a Women at Risk program in 1988 to help female refugee claimants who lacked "the normal protection of a family unit and who find themselves in precarious situations where the local authorities cannot ensure their safety." Further, in 1993, Canada officially recognized gender as a ground of persecution for the purpose of a refugee claim.

The issue of sexual harassment entered the feminist lexicon in 1974, after an American woman, Carmita Wood, quit her job because of ongoing sexual advances by her boss. When she was denied unemployment benefits, a group of feminists at Cornell University supported her argument that her boss's actions forced her to quit. Wood's claim was rejected, but the term "sexual harassment" gained acceptance.

In Canada, sexual harassment was prohibited under provincial human rights codes and, in 1983, the Canadian Human Rights Act was amended to prohibit sexual harassment in workplaces under federal jurisdiction. Prohibitions against sexual harassment remained ineffective, however, until 1987 when the Supreme Court of Canada released a ground-breaking ruling on sexual harassment. Bonnie Robichaud, employed by the Department of National Defence in 1979, reported that she had been coerced into sexual activity with her supervisor. The Federal Court of Appeal had ruled that although Robichaud had been sexually harassed, the Department of National Defence was not liable for the contravention of Robichaud's rights under the Canadian Human Rights Act. The Supreme Court, in its unanimous ruling, stated that employers are considered liable for sexual harassment in the workplace.

THE CHARTER OF RIGHTS AND FREEDOMS

Prime Minister John Diefenbaker proclaimed Canada's first Bill of Rights in 1960, a decade after the United Nations adopted the *Universal Declaration of Human Rights*. Canada's bill set out to guarantee, among other liberties, equality before the law based on race and sex. As Liberal cabinet minister July LaMarsh aptly described it, the bill was "framed in awkward, uninspiring language, clouded by ambiguity, suffering fatally from being just another Act passed by both Houses of Parliament, and subject to amendment by ordinary procedure at any time."[23]

It was a weak document, in other words, and women still had to fight to secure their rights. It was only after the Front de libération des femmes organized a public protest in 1971, for example, that Quebec women were allowed to be called as jurors. The following year, women in Newfoundland and Labrador were included in jury selections for the first time. Meanwhile, amendments to Quebec's Civil Code in 1969 improved the province's matrimonial regime and established the full legal capacity of both partners. The institution of marriage still had a long way to go, however, as far as feminists were concerned.

In 1973, upon the end of her marriage to a violent husband, Irene Murdoch, an Alberta farm wife, was denied a half-interest in the farm she and her husband had built over twenty-five years. The contribution of Murdoch towards the couple's 480-acre ranch was viewed by courts as simply the fulfilment of a farm wife's "normal" duties, not as an equal partner's investment in joint property. Even after appealing the case to the Supreme Court in 1975, Murdoch was unsuccessful. However, Supreme Court Justice Bora Laskin issued a historic dissenting opinion, which, along with lobbying from women's groups, helped form the basis for provincial family law reforms that soon required that assets acquired during the course of a marriage be split equally upon divorce.

In 1971, Jeanette Corbiere Lavell, a member of the Wikwemikong band, married a non-Aboriginal man and was no longer a status Indian entitled to benefits according to section 12(1)(b) of the Indian Act. Such women could no longer live on reserves and they lost the right to own land or inherit family property. Their children were not entitled to status and, like their mothers, lost their benefits and standing in the community. Without status, they could not be buried in cemeteries with their ancestors. Lavell believed this was discriminatory under the Canadian Bill of Rights, since the Indian Act did not disqualify Indian men who married non-Aboriginal women.

Meanwhile, Yvonne Bédard from the Six Nations Indian Reserve in Brantford, Ontario, had taken a similar case to the courts. She had been evicted after returning to her reserve upon her separation from a non-status Indian. Although a Federal Court of Appeal initially ruled in Lavell's favour, the Supreme Court of Canada struck it down. It then ruled jointly in Lavell and Bedard's cases in 1973, stating that Canada's Bill of Rights did not "forbid inequality within a group or class by itself, by reason of sex." The discriminatory provisions remained. Lavell, a founding member of the Ontario Native Women's Association in 1972, was the organization's president from 1974 to 1975. She was also a vice-president of the Native Women's Association of Canada.

Then, in 1979, Sandra Lovelace, of the Tobique reserve in New Brunswick, who had also lost her status upon marriage to a non-status man, brought her discrimination case to the United Nations International Human Rights Commission. It ruled in her favour and found Canada in breach of the International Covenant on Civil and Political Rights. In 1985, section 12 of the Indian Act was repealed as part of bill C-31 and women were allowed to retain their Indian status upon marriage to non-status men.

Many legal changes during the 1970s and 1980s ended discriminatory laws and regulations, including those governing pension plans and other programs. Unemployment Insurance (UI) now included maternity leave but, as Stella Bliss found out, UI regulations placed pregnant women in a Catch-22. Bliss had been fired for pregnancy-related reasons shortly before giving birth — an act for which no legal recourse existed at the time. After her baby was born, Bliss was unable to find work and she applied for unemployment insurance benefits. Bliss had worked long enough to qualify for unemployment benefits, but the Unemployment Insurance Commission denied Bliss benefits because she had been pregnant when she was fired and, under the Act, was subject to the act's maternity provisions, not the "regular" benefits. However, Bliss didn't meet the stricter criteria for maternity benefits and her claim was denied. She took her case to the Federal Court of Appeal. The judge determined that the unemployment regulations were discriminatory. But he ruled that because they discriminated against pregnant people and not all women, the regulations did not contravene Canada's Bill of Rights. The Supreme Court upheld the ruling, stating, "Any inequality between the sexes in this area is not created by legislation, but by nature."

Both the Bill of Rights and the all-male Supreme Court stood in the way of a more inclusive interpretation of equality. Canadian jurisprudence showed clearly in the cases of Lavell, Lovelace, Bliss and Murdoch that the 1960 Bill of Rights did not protect women from the effects of discriminatory laws.

And so, when Prime Minster Pierre Trudeau vowed to patriate Canada's constitution in the late 1970s and create a charter of rights and freedoms, women were determined to ensure that strong and unalterable equality rights would be enshrined to protect women and other minorities from discriminatory laws. Unfortunately, according to legal experts Marilou McPhedran and Susan Bazilli, writing in the *International Review of Constitutionalism*, Trudeau's initial proposed equality clause simply "echoed the empty guarantees in the Canadian Bill of Rights that had failed Canadian women."[24]

At first, Ottawa tried to brush off the women who wanted strong equality measures. After NAC made a presentation before the Special Joint Committee of the Senate and of the House of Commons on the Constitution of Canada in November 1980, committee co-chair Senator Harry Hays said to presenters, "I want to thank you girls for your presentation. We're honoured to have you here. But I wonder why you don't have anything in here for babies and children? All you girls are going to be working and who's going to look after them?"

Over the next few months, women's tenacity was directed toward improving section 15, which would become the equality rights clause in the Canadian Charter of Rights and Freedoms. Feminists fought to ensure that not only equality "under the law" was guaranteed for women and other minorities, but they also called for equality "before the law." Importantly, they also fought for a guarantee of "equal protection and benefit of the law." Such specificity was required since courts often ignored discrimination.

Much of the lobbying for more substantive wording in section 15 occurred under the auspices of the Canadian Advisory Council on the Status of Women (CACSW). However, the minister responsible for the status of women at the time, Lloyd Axworthy, was said to be less than enthusiastic about the Advisory Council's decision to step beyond a purely advisory role. The trust between the Axworthy and women's groups fractured when Axworthy made it known to executive members of CACSW that he wanted an upcoming February 1981 conference on women and the constitution postponed. Eighteen days before the scheduled conference, the CACSW executive called off the conference while its chairperson, Doris Anderson, was out of town. Anderson resigned in protest upon her return and grassroots women vowed to meet independently.

Meanwhile, federal Attorney General Jean Chrétien had agreed to changes in the equality rights clause that would create "an opening for non-enumerated or analogous grounds of discrimination," as McPhedran and Bazilli put it. In other words, later courts could "read in" forms of discrimination not specified in the draft charter.

On February 14, 1981, 1,300 women met in Ottawa to consolidate their constitutional demands under the banner of the Ad Hoc Committee of Canadian Women on the Constitution. Members of Parliament from the three major political parties joined legal experts, CACSW members and activists on Parliament Hill to hash out the women's agenda for constitutional reform. Lawyer Marilou McPhedran, activist Linda Ryan-Nye and New Brunswick Advisory Council Chairperson Madeleine LeBlanc co-chaired the Saturday event. The women's efforts led to demands for a second equality clause in the Charter, a clause that would stipulate (just in case there was any room for doubt left in section 15) that all of the rights in the charter were intended to benefit men and women equally. In order for the new section 28 to be included, women had to garner promises from premiers that the provinces wouldn't subject section 28 to the "override clause," an escape clause that would allow provinces to opt out of sections of the Charter. They succeeded, and afterward, constitutional activist Linda Ryan-Nye said, "Twenty-eight was a helluva lot to lose, because to put it under the override would have been to entrench inequality. But it was not a helluva lot to win."

Section 28 of the Canadian Charter of Rights and Freedoms states, "Notwithstanding anything in this Charter, the rights and freedoms referred to in it are guaranteed equally to male and female persons." Section 15 of the Charter states," Every individual is equal before and under the law and has the right to the equal protection and equal benefit of the law without discrimination and, in particular, without discrimination based on race, national or ethnic origin, colour, religion, sex, age or mental or physical disability."

The Charter ushered in an era of "substantive equality." This concept goes a step further than "formal equality," which assumes that equality means only treating all persons alike. Because not all individuals or groups are identically situated, a formal equality model may not be substantive enough to address discrimination and inequality. Substantive equality recognizes that equality requires the accommodation of differences, not simply equal treatment. Substantive equality acknowledges that laws themselves, as well as those who have traditionally interpreted them, have historically perpetuated inequalities.

The significance of the Charter as a tool for broadening the concept of equality in Canada cannot be overstated. Supreme Court Justice Claire L'Heureux-Dubé told a conference on the National Association of Women in the Law in 1997 that, "Equality is beginning to inform the interpretation and application of legislation and the development of common law principles, even outside the arena of constitutionally based discrimination claims. Substantive equality principles are proving to be helpful tools for addressing obstacles to full access to justice by women and others in all areas of the law."

Due to women's efforts, the Charter is a stronger tool of justice than it would have otherwise been. The language in the Charter signalled to courts that they had the power to order results-based remedies. As a result, the Charter has been widely used by the courts to strike down discriminatory laws, to "read in" grounds of discrimination not initially listed and to re-tool the constructs of justice.

In response to the coming into effect of the Charter, the Women's Legal Education and Action Fund (LEAF) was established on April 19, 1985, by feminist lawyers to coordinate women's legal response to the Charter. It was founded to promote women's legal rights under the

Charter and has intervened in applicable Supreme Court cases affecting women's equality rights.

When she applied to Dalhousie Law School in 1954, Bertha Wilson was advised by the law school dean that crocheting might make a better pastime than studying law. Fortunately, she did not heed his advice and, in 1982, Wilson became the first female justice appointed to the Supreme Court of Canada. Over her nine years on the Supreme Court, Wilson often argued for an inclusive interpretation of equality rights.

In 1982, Justice Bertha Wilson became the first woman appointed to the Supreme Court of Canada.

One of the cases for which Wilson is best known involved a precedent of self-defence based on what is referred to as battered woman syndrome. The case involved a Manitoba woman, Angelique Lavallee, who had been assaulted by her partner, Kevin Rust, for a period of years. Lavallee testified in court that one night, Rust handed her a gun. During an argument, Rust assaulted Lavallee and told her that she would have to kill him or else he would kill her. As he was leaving the room, Lavallee shot and killed Rust. She was charged with second-degree murder. Her lawyer argued that she was not guilty as she acted in self-defence. A jury acquitted her.

The case was appealed to the Supreme Court and Wilson, writing for the majority in 1990, noted the court's obligation to consider the social context of the violence in which Lavallee lived, not only the immediate circumstances of Lavallee's action. Thus, the Supreme Court determined that it was reasonable for Lavallee to conclude that her life was in danger, and it upheld her jury acquittal. The case represented a significant departure from how the court defined the legal concept of "reasonable behaviour."

Wilson's rulings "helped shape not only Canada's legal landscape but also, indeed, our sense of who we are as Canadians," according to L'Heureux-Dubé, writing in the preface to the book *Justice Bertha Wilson*. Another groundbreaking jurist, L'Heureux-Dubé was the first woman from Quebec and the second woman in history to be appointed to the Supreme Court of Canada, in 1987.[25]

In 1989, Beverley McLachlin was appointed to the Supreme Court of Canada. McLachlin gained a reputation as a libertarian for her role in striking down the offence of spreading false news in R. *v.* Zundel. Among her controversial decisions was her opinion in R. *v.* Seaboyer, a ruling that struck down Canada's existing rape shield law. The ruling determined that the law violated the right to a fair trial of a person accused of sexual assault. In the decision R. *v.* Sharpe, the Supreme Court supported the upholding of Canada's child pornography law, but writing for the majority, McLachlin wrote that "imaginative works" intended for private use should be excluded. In 2000, McLachlin became Canada's first female chief justice.

In 1995, Louise Arbour was appointed to head a commission of inquiry into allegations of prisoner abuse at the Prison for Women in Kingston, Ontario. The next year, Arbour was appointed Chief Prosecutor of the International Criminal Tribunal for Rwanda and the International Criminal Tribunal for the former Yugoslavia. In this role, she indicted Serbian president Slobodan Milosevic for war crimes, the first time a serving head of state was prosecuted by an international court. She also oversaw the first prosecution in which sexual assault was tried as a crime against humanity. In 1999, Arbour was appointed to the Supreme Court of Canada.

THE FIGHT FOR ABORTION

Justice Minister Pierre Trudeau's 1968–1969 Criminal Law Amendment Act legalized homosexual acts between consenting adults and also legalized birth control. Abortion was legalized in some circumstances; however, the law required women seeking abortions to plead their case before a hospital therapeutic abortion committee made up of doctors and a psychiatrist. This was widely viewed by women as a patronizing hindrance to their autonomy and freedom.

So strong was the opposition to the committee model that during a 1968 debate on Trudeau's bill at the University of Toronto, Judy LaMarsh, who had by then left politics, told the audience, "If I were pregnant I would prefer a dirty kitchen with a spoon and knife" (a reference to illegal abortion) rather than a therapeutic abortion committee. She and other feminists were adamant that abortion should be strictly a matter between a woman and her doctor.

Anger over the abortion law transformed women's fury into the pivotal event known as the Abortion Caravan. Seventeen women from a Vancouver women's group called the Women's Caucus, set out on a May 1970 road trip to confront Pierre Trudeau, who was by then prime minister, and have the law changed. Taking their cue from the On-To-Ottawa Trek, a protest of poor conditions in Depression-era relief camps in 1935, the Abortion Caravan began with two cars and a van that had the slogan "Smash Capitalism" on its side. A coffin, perched on top of the van, symbolized the deaths of Canadian women as a result of illegal abortions.[26]

By the time the women had reached Alberta, reporters were listening and reporting on their cause. At each stop along the way, the caravan protesters performed feminist theatre in the evening and listened as local women shared their stories about illegal abortions. According to caravan participant Marcy Cohen, interviewed by Judy

Rebick in *Ten Thousand Roses: The Making of a Feminist Revolution*, "The public meeting would inevitably end up with wrenching horror stories and tears … We were ready to get arrested once we got to Ottawa." Many women had never spoken about their abortions before, and these discussion forums cemented the philosophical underpinnings of the abortion movement.

By the time it reached Ottawa, the Abortion Caravan had attracted five hundred supporters. At a meeting on Parliamentary Hill, recalled caravan participant Margo Dunn, "Henry Morgentaler spoke and was hissed for not being radical enough."[27] On Friday, May 8, the protesters descended on Trudeau's residence on Sussex Drive after failing to find a government representative on Parliament Hill to meet with them. Then, on Monday, May 11, thirty-six protesters set out to occupy the parliamentary gallery. They borrowed nylons and gloves and wore dresses — a tactic to distract security guards from finding the chains stuffed in their purses.

The night before, huddled in an abandoned school that was their headquarters, the women debated the issue of chaining themselves to the gallery and facing arrest. One of the women, Doris Power, who was in her eighth month of a pregnancy that she did not plan, was living on welfare. "I can see for some of you it's hard to make a choice because it makes a real difference to your lives if you go to jail or not," she told the group. "For me, there isn't any difference. I'm in chains wherever I am, jail or out."[28]

That afternoon, NDP MP Andrew Brewin asked Minister of Justice John Turner if he would consider reviewing the abortion law; he declined. Once they were all seated, the protesters chained themselves to the gallery, a nod to suffragists who had chained themselves to the British Parliament. Shortly before three o'clock, one of the protesters began reciting the group's demands and, on cue, the others joined in. Some of the chains didn't hold, but the women managed to close down the House of Commons for forty-five minutes — a first in its 103-year history — while security guards hauled them out. Outside, about eighty women wearing black head scarves circled the Centennial flame on Parliament Hill, carrying the coffin. A placard on which the words of Canada's abortion law were written was burned.

Ten women were taken into police custody, although none were charged. In the end, national media coverage of the Abortion Caravan bolstered the movement for abortion and helped to make the women's movement an unstoppable force. The caravan also demanded that free birth control be provided in women's community health centres.

The following month, in June 1970, Dr. Henry Morgentaler was arrested for the first time for performing abortions in his Montreal clinic. Over the next six years, Morgentaler was charged three times for violating Canada's abortion law. Each time, he was acquitted by a jury. In 1974, an Ontario Court of Appeal overturned a jury acquittal of Morgentaler, sentencing him to eighteen months. He appealed the ruling to the Supreme Court, was refused, and in 1975 served ten months in prison. The following year, Canada's justice minister set aside Morgentaler's conviction after the Criminal Code was amended to disallow appeal courts from overturning jury acquittals. A new trial was ordered and once again, Morgentaler was acquitted.

Until the mid-1980s, Morgentaler continued to flout the law, expanding the number of abortion clinics he operated across Canada. He and other physicians who worked at his clinics were repeatedly arrested. Morgentaler is also credited with the development of an abortion method, provided in his clinics, that was safer than that performed in hospitals.

The Canadian Association for the Repeal of the Abortion Law (CARAL) had formed in 1974 to lobby government to decriminalize abortion. During the early 1980s, the pro-choice movement gained momentum and tens of thousands of pro-choice supporters marched in the streets of major cities to protest Canada's abortion law and to raise money for Henry Morgentaler's legal defence. CARAL changed its name to the Canadian Abortion Rights Action League in 1980. Norma Scarborough, a founding member of CARAL, was English Canada's national face for abortion rights. During the Second World War, Scarborough had been in the Canadian Women's Army Corps, and one of her colleagues bled to death after having an illegal abortion. The experience grounded Scarborough's conviction that abortion should be legal. CARAL Ottawa member Anne Burnett said of Scarborough: "She talked quietly but forcefully to people, and they listened."[29]

Most sections of the Charter were in effect in 1983 when Morgentaler was charged with unlawfully procuring miscarriages in his Toronto clinic. He was convicted. But upon appeal, the constitutionality of Canada's abortion law was ultimately decided by the Supreme Court of Canada on January 28, 1988. It struck down section 251 of the Criminal Code as a violation of the constitutional right to life, liberty and security of the person under section 7 of the Charter. Therapeutic abortion committees, it ruled, caused delays and therefore threatened pregnant women's health. In her decision, Justice Bertha Wilson wrote: "Liberty in a free and democratic society does not require the state to approve the personal decisions made by its citizens; it does, however, require the state to respect them."

In 1989, men in Ontario, Manitoba and Quebec took former girlfriends to court, seeking injunctions against the women's planned abortions. None were successful, though in the case of Chantal Daigle of Quebec, a hastily convened Supreme Court had to be called to quash a lower court injunction that ruled in her ex-boyfriend's favour.

Then, in November 1989, the Progressive Conservative government of Brian Mulroney introduced Bill C-43, an act that would prohibit abortion unless a doctor determined that a pregnancy threatened a woman's health. The bill passed third reading in the House of Commons by a vote of 140 to 131. However, in a dramatic move, Progressive Conservative female senators joined pro-choice Liberal senators and voted against the bill on January 31, 1991. The vote was a tie, forty-three to forty-three. Under Senate rules, a tie vote is a negative vote. Conservative pro-choice senators Pat Carney, Janice Johnson and Mira Spivak were among those who voted nay. It was the first time in thirty years the Senate had defeated a government bill.

VIOLENCE AGAINST WOMEN

Consciousness-raising groups in the 1960s and early 1970s provided a safe place for women to share their personal stories, including those dealing with violence. In doing so, many women's lives were politicized. As a result of women's discussions with other women, a greater awareness emerged about the extent to which violence affected women's lives.

Wife battering was a crime for which men were generally absolved

Abortion Stats

Source: Hennessy's Index (www.policyalternatives.ca/publications/commentary/abortion-and-womens-rights)

 15.9%
Canadian hospitals that offer accessible abortion services – that's only one in every six hospitals in Canada. In PEI, women must leave the province to access a safe abortion.

 68,000
Women estimated to die every year from unsafe abortions around the world. Most (97%) occur in developing countries. Legal abortions in developed countries have a death rate of less than 1 in 100,000.

of responsibility and for which victims were often faulted. Centuries-old beliefs, quoted in British courts in the 1800s, suggested that a husband was permitted to use a switch, or broomstick, to "correct" his wife as long as it wasn't thicker than his thumb. This allowance is thought to have informed the expression "rule of thumb." Although not enshrined in law, an unspoken tolerance for wife assault meant that police rarely charged violent husbands. In an effort to change such beliefs and to provide safety to victims, feminists lobbied for the creation of women's crisis shelters.

The first shelters for women in violent relationships opened in Canada in 1973. They were in Vancouver (Transition House), in Langley, B.C. (Ishtar), Calgary (Oasis House, now Calgary Women's Emergency Shelter), Saskatoon (Interval House) and Toronto (Interval House). By 1975, eighteen women's shelters were in operation and another fifty-seven opened between 1975 and 1979. Providing shelter and counselling in a safe environment addressed a problem that had affected one in ten women who were married or living in a common-law relationship with a male partner.

Women's advocates also worked closely with justice officials and law enforcement agencies in the 1980s to ensure police laid charges when women called for help. They also worked to create treatment programs for offenders of wife abuse and to develop educational programs for judges, police and lawyers so that they would treat the crime more seriously.

Wife abuse was still considered a private matter, but the public response began to undergo a major transformation in the early 1980s. "Starting with a directive from the federal Solicitor General to the RCMP, police forces across the country implemented 'mandatory' or 'zero tolerance' charging policies in cases of intimate partner violence."[30] In 1982, provinces began to direct police departments to lay charges in cases of wife abuse, removing the onus from the women to have charges laid.

A turning point in public awareness came when Margaret Mitchell, NDP MP for Vancouver East, stood up in the House of Commons on May 12, 1982, to address a report on wife abuse issued by the federal standing committee on health, welfare and social affairs. After informing the House that one in ten women had been battered, several Liberal and Conservative male MPs erupted in laughter. "I don't beat my wife, do you?" one MP was heard to say. "This is no laughing matter," Mitchell responded. Public outrage against the laughing MPs turned the event into a catalyst that helped change the belief that wife abuse was not serious.

Shelters were only part of the solution. Many women stayed in violent relationships due to economic factors, as Nancy Janovicek noted in *No Place to Go: Local Histories of the Battered Women's Movement*. The reasons were often more complicated for Aboriginal women, Janovicek wrote. "Racism, unfair child welfare practices and discrimination under the Indian Act made it even more difficult for Aboriginal women to leave ... Confusing and inconsistent jurisdiction over services for Aboriginal people restricted women's access to welfare."[31] Eventually there would be three dozen Aboriginal-run emergency shelters and transition houses in six provinces.

In response to demands from women's advocates, specialized domestic violence courts were set up. The Winnipeg Family Violence Court was the first such court, established in 1990.[32] Family violence courts ensured that judges and other justice officials familiar with the dynamics of violence would preside over wife- and child-abuse cases. The specialized domestic violence courts were intended to provide an opportunity for early intervention for low-risk offenders, to follow procedures for vigorous prosecution of more serious cases, and to try to ensure rehabilitation and treatment for offenders.

In 1988, the federal government pledged to spend $40 million over four years on wife battering research, education and assistance. The federal Panel on Violence Against Women in 1991 made further recommendations for reducing violent crimes against women. It developed hundreds of recommendations geared to police and justice officials, law schools, unions, employers, human rights commissions, media organizations, provincial governments — even advertising agencies. The panel also conducted a survey of 420 women, which found that for one-quarter of women assaulted, their partners explicitly threatened to kill them.[33]

In August 1993, section 264 of the Criminal Code was amended to create the new offence of criminal harassment. Commonly known as "stalking," the law was a specific response to violence against women, though it applies to anyone experiencing persistent harassment. Further changes were made in 1997 to make the violation of a protective court order an aggravating factor for sentencing purposes.[34]

Although many women's advocates sought the introduction of specific provisions in the Criminal Code to distinguish intimate assault from other forms of assault, this was not accomplished.

Rape was another example of male violence for which victims were often blamed. In Canada, an accused rapist could use the defence that he had an "honest belief" that the complainant had consented to have sex with him. Similar laws existed in many countries. To protest rape in Germany and Belgium in 1973, women began to organize annual Take Back the Night marches. By 1979, Take Back the Night marches had become fall occurrences on many Canadian streets.

In Canada in 1971 there were 2,107 cases of rape reported to police. Half of them were deemed "founded" by the police and 119 of those accused were charged. In response to the perceived lack of justice for rape victims, three women started Vancouver Rape Relief in 1973. It was first housed in the basement of one of its founders. The next year, Toronto women established a rape crisis centre. By 1979, centres in twelve other Ontario cities established services to provide counselling to rape victims. In 1980, the Canadian Association of Sexual Assault Centres (CASAC) was formed to enable advocates to discuss common concerns and to lobby government to reform sexual assault laws and improve police practices.

A victory came in 1983 with the passage of Bill C-127, a law that redefined rape and indecent assault as sexual assault. The purpose of the change was to emphasize that the offence was essentially a crime of violence, not strictly one of sexual conduct. The new law created three tiers of offences: sexual assault — punishable by a maximum of ten years imprisonment; sexual assault with a weapon or causing bodily harm — which carried a maximum sentence of fourteen years; and aggravated sexual assault — punishable by a maximum of life imprisonment. Before the new law was enacted, a husband could not be charged with sexual assault if the complainant was his wife. The new law also stipulated that penetration was no longer a requirement for sexual assault to have occurred. Prior to Bill C-127, the penalty for indecent assault against a male had been twice as high as for indecent assault against a female.

From the feminist movement, society also gained a widened understanding of the impact of childhood sexual abuse. Often, victims were vulnerable youth in institutions, such as Aboriginal children in residential schools who were abused by caregivers or teachers. Aboriginal women were three times more likely than non-Aboriginal women to experience sexual assault. Echoing the sentiment that vulnerable children are targeted for sexual abuse, a DisAbled Women's Network of Ontario 1987 report concluded the "the most danger-ous place for a disabled girl or woman to be was in her own home."

Under Bill C-127, women's sexual histories could no longer be liberally scrutinized by defence lawyers in an attempt to discredit a rape victim's court testimony. In 1991, this rape shield provision was struck down by the Supreme Court of Canada in the case of R. *v.* Seaboyer. The court ruled the law was a violation of an accused's right to a fair trial. After holding consultations with women's groups and women's legal experts, Bill C-49 was introduced by Justice Minister Kim Campbell in 1992. The new law stipulated conditions under which victims past sexual conduct could be introduced during a trial. The new rape shield law also refined the definition of consent to a sexual act. It also restricted the defence that allowed men accused of sexual assault to argue that they had an honest but mistaken belief that the complainant consented.

Further changes followed. In 1995, Bishop Hubert O'Connor was convicted of rape and indecent assault involving two Aboriginal young women in his care while he was principal of a residential school near Williams Lake, B.C. It was in the 1960s when the assaults occurred. During his trial, O'Connor's counsel obtained a pre-trial order requiring that the Crown disclose the complainants' full medical, counselling and school records. Women's advocates were angered that the person in charge of creating some those personal records was the person intending to use them to discredit the women's testimonies. In response, Bill C-46, passed in 1996, set limits on the conditions under which a complainant may be required to produce personal counselling records.

During the decade that followed the passage of Bill C-127 in 1983, there was a 100 percent increase in the number of sexual assault reports received by police in Canada. This may have been due to improved social attitudes towards victims of sexual assault, to greater awareness of the new law or an increase in actual assaults. There were 30,735 "founded" sexual assaults reported to police in Canada in 1997. The number of sexual offences reported to the police then declined by 33 percent between 1993 and 1999; however, report rates remained 50 percent higher than they were pre–Bill C-127.

A national survey in 1999 found that 78 percent of sexual assaults were not reported to police. According to a Canadian Panel on Violence Against Women survey, 17 percent of women had experienced sexual abuse by a family member before age sixteen; 40 percent of women reported at least one experience of some form of sexual assault by age sixteen. The survey found that 81 percent of perpetrators were known to the victims, with 38 percent being identified as husbands, common-law partners or boyfriends.

At a time when many rape victims felt too shamed to come forward, a woman known as "Jane Doe" demanded police accountability and in so doing, made history. In 1986, Jane Doe was sexually assaulted by a man who was known to Toronto police as the Balcony Rapist. When Doe discovered there had been four other balcony rapes in her community prior to her assault, she sued the board of commissioners for the Toronto police for not warning residents, and won. Her civil suit claimed police negligence and further claimed that police inaction was a violation of her Charter equality rights as well as an infringement of her Charter right to security of the person. On July 3, 1998, Ontario Justice Jean MacFarland ruled in her favour and Doe was awarded $220,000 in damages. The judge ruled that the police owed a duty of care to the women in Doe's neighbourhood and that they "utterly" failed in their duty to protect these women.

In 1984, the federal Committee on Sexual Offences Against

Children and Youth, known as the Badgley Committee, made fifty-two recommendations for legal reforms, public education and child welfare changes to protect child sexual assault victims. In 1988, Bill C-15 was passed and brought with it greater protection to child witnesses/victims. It also created a new offence, sexual touching, designed to enhance the prosecution of sexual abuse perpetrators.

After a flood of reports of child sexual abuse by former residents of Newfoundland's Mount Cashel Orphanage, the issue of the sexual abuse of children came crashing to the public forefront in Canada. The courts eventually ordered the assets of the Foundation of Christian Brothers sold to compensate the victims, who were to receive between $20,000 and $600,000 in compensation. A 1989 commission headed by former Supreme Court of Ontario judge Samuel Hughes investigated the cover-up of sexual abuse that had been previously made. Nine members of the Christian Brothers of Ireland in Canada and five civilian staff were convicted of eighty-eight counts of physical and sexual abuse.

Laws on violence, however, can only be applied once a crime has been committed. This was underscored on December 6, 1989, when a former student entered École Polytechnique in Montreal and killed fourteen young women using a semi-automatic rifle. The killer, Marc Lépine, wrote in a suicide note that feminists had ruined his life. As his vendetta, he entered an engineering classroom and shot all nine women in the room, killing six. When the rampage was over, fourteen women were dead and ten other women, as well as four men, were injured. Lépine then fatally shot himself. For women, it was particularly chilling that Lépine targeted female engineering students — symbols of women's entry into non-traditional occupations. In the outpouring of grief and anger that followed the killings, women, including female family members of those killed in the Montreal

Massacre, as it came to be known, led a lobby to make Canada's gun control laws stricter. Half a million signatures demanding stricter gun control in Canada were gathered. In polls taken, women supported stricter gun control at a rate that was 22.8 percent higher than men did. One of the survivors of the massacre, former engineering student, Heidi Rathjen, became a leader in Canada's gun control lobby.

After the Progressive Conservative government was defeated in 1993, Liberal justice minister Allan Rock picked up the gun control portfolio and a new gun control bill, Bill C-68, passed the House of Commons in November 1995. However, the bill would not have received Senate approval if Progressive Conservative female senators had not crossed party lines to give the bill the votes it needed to pass the Tory-dominated Senate. In the end, 75 percent of female senators backed Bill C-68, compared to 55 percent of male senators.

THE PORNOGRAPHY DEBATE

On November 22, 1982, an anonymous group calling itself the Wimmin's Fire Brigade firebombed an outlet of Red Hot Video, a Vancouver pornography outlet with a reputation for distributing violent pornography. The perpetrators claimed in a statement the attack was an act of self-defence on behalf of women and children. The event intensified a nation-wide debate about whether pornography was harmful to women. The firebombing followed the release of filmmaker Bonnie Sherr Klein's provocative documentary about pornography, *Not a Love Story*, by the National Film Board in 1982.

Many feminists believed than violent pornography was linked to sexist attitudes as well as to acts of sexual violence against women. In the 1980s, the rise of home videos and expanded cable television increased people's access to sexually explicit movies in the home. After the equality provisions of the Charter came into effect as of April

17, 1985, it was only a matter of time before the Charter's freedom of expression guarantees in section 2(b) collided with section 15's equality rights.

A lobby of women's organizations asked the federal government to alter the Criminal Code's definition of pornography distribution by adopting a harm-based approach. The existing law, adopted in the 1950s, relied on courts to determine whether "community standards" were exceeded to determine whether material distributed was obscene. Section 163(8) of the Criminal Code stated that "any publication, a dominant characteristic of which is the undue exploitation of sex, or of sex and any one or more of the following subjects: namely, crime, horror, cruelty and violence, shall be deemed to be obscene." In fact, the definition was viewed as an improvement over a previous law that defined obscenity as any material deemed likely to "corrupt morals." Still, many feminists found the focus on "undue exploitation of sex" to be problematic.

Organizations like the newly formed Canadian Coalition Against Media Pornography did not object to sexually explicit material, but wanted access to violent pornography restricted. Feminist critics of Canada's obscenity regime argued that community "tolerance" for pornography didn't mean that pornography was harmless. They further claimed that giving judges — who were, by and large white, privileged men — the power to determine community standards for sexually explicit material was a biased approach. In other words, according to Richard Jochelson and Kirsten Kramar, authors of *Sex and the Supreme Court: Obscenity and Indecency Laws in Canada,* the obscenity provisions "empowered the judiciary to limit free expression on the basis of whether or not the courts (speaking on behalf of society) determined the exploitation to be undue."[35]

The pornography debate in Canada culminated with the case of

Donald Butler, a Winnipeg video store owner who was convicted in 1987 with distributing pornography. Butler appealed the conviction, arguing that his freedom of expression rights under the Charter were violated by Canada's obscenity law. He sought to have the law struck down.

The Women's Legal Education and Action Fund (LEAF) intervened at the Supreme Court hearing in the Butler case. LEAF's argument "was that pornography is a form of sex discrimination that affects individual women and women as a group and that society's social interest in equality outweighs any protection to free expression guaranteed under section 2(b) of the Charter."[36] LEAF's position was that degrading and dehumanizing pornography caused harm to women in its production and desensitized viewers' tolerance of violence towards women. Therefore, it reasoned, violent and degrading pornography should be viewed as a threat to women's equality.

The view was controversial. Anti-pornography feminists faced criticism by civil libertarians, as well as by others who didn't believe that pornography depicting violence was necessarily harmful. Anti-pornography feminists were also characterized by some gay and lesbian activists as "anti-sex" and "pro-censorship." Because gay men and lesbians faced discrimination because of societal beliefs about proper sexual expressions, many gays and lesbians believed that Canada would be better off with fewer restrictions on sexual materials.

In 1992, the Supreme Court ruled that Canada's obscenity laws were a reasonable limit on freedom of speech and Butler's conviction was upheld. The court stated that equality was one element of a proper functioning society and that sexually explicit expression was a protected form of speech under the Charter's freedom of expression guarantees. The Supreme Court had, in its ruling in Butler, created a three-tiered test to be used in obscenity cases. Tier one covered materials with explicit sex with violence; tier two was explicit sex which subjects people to treatment that is degrading or dehumanizing; and the third tier was materials with explicit sex without violence or degrading or dehumanizing treatment.

Meanwhile, gay and lesbian bookstore owners had begun to complain that erotic materials they attempted to import for sale were being routinely seized at the border. Since the same materials were sometimes sold in non-gay bookstores that did not have their shipments seized, the LGBT-run stores charged that Canada Customs officials had discriminated against them. In 1988, Little Sister's Book and Art Emporium and the British Columbia Civil Liberties Association challenged Canada Customs over its seizure of gay and lesbian materials. They argued that banning the importation of obscene material was unconstitutional because it put the onus on the importer to disprove obscenity.

LEAF was displeased to learn that the new "Butler test" was being used to seize gay and lesbian materials intended for gay and lesbian bookstores. LEAF and anti-censorship gay and lesbian advocates then issued a joint news release that "unanimously condemned the use of the Butler decision to justify the discriminatory use of laws to harass and intimidate lesbians and gays and sex trade workers." In 2000, the Supreme Court determined that customs officials had been discriminatory in the seizures and that the bookstore owners had experienced differential treatment. The court did uphold Canada Customs right to prevent importing obscene materials but struck down the reverse onus requirement that made importers prove material was not obscene.

THE END OF THE TWENTIETH CENTURY

A cluster of political and global economic trends in the final decade of the twentieth century served to diminish the visibility and the effectiveness of the feminist movement in Canada.

Primary among those trends was a focus on fiscal policy over social policy development. By the early 1990s, governments started to emphasize deficit and debt reduction. There was a change from providing core funding to equality-seeking organizations to providing short-term funding for projects. This shift was signalled when, under Liberal Prime Minister Jean Chrétien, Ottawa shut down the Canadian Advisory Council on the Status of Women in 1995.

Another important voice for women had been Studio D, the women's division within the National Film Board of Canada. Set up to mark the United Nations declaration of International Women's Year in 1975, Studio D, under the direction of Kathleen Shannon, was the world's first government-funded film studio in the world dedicated to women filmmakers. Studio D films won many awards for their acclaimed production of feminist films dealing with social issues, peace, sexuality and women's history. Among them were the anti-nuclear documentary *If You Love This Planet, Not a Love Story* and *Forbidden Love: The Unashamed Stories of Lesbian Lives*. In 1996, as a result of sweeping federal budget cuts, Studio D was closed.

In 1996, Joan Grant-Cummings became the thirteenth president of NAC and the second woman of colour elected to the post. It was a difficult time for the organization. The Secretary of State women's program budget was being pared down by Ottawa and NAC's funding was reduced from 1993 onward. A succession of ongoing federal cuts undermined the effectiveness and influence of many women's advocacy groups during this time. Without operational funds needed to conduct research, write reports and consult with members across the country, NAC's ability to mobilize member groups weakened, and, as a result, the visibility of the Canadian women's movement decreased. Thus, the country's most influential feminist organization had largely ceased its operations by the late 1990s, and other feminist organizations were forced to close due to funding cuts during the final years of the century.

The federal government also ended the Canada Assistance Plan, a fifty-fifty cost sharing arrangement Ottawa had with the provinces to fund specified programs including welfare, education and public housing initiatives. The elimination of the Canada Assistance Plan in 1995 pushed greater responsibility for social programs to the provinces and resulted in a move away from national standards and even national programs. "It was the Liberals in the 1990s that moved from federal transfers to the provinces with conditions attached — that specified how the money was to be spent — to completely unconditional transfers that can be spent on anything and with no accountability," according to feminist legal expert Shelagh Day. "This single move has turned Canada's social program infrastructure into a creaky, diminished and uneven patchwork."[1]

Canada's system of public social programs and services had been one of the foundations for the advancement of women. After the conditions attached to federal transfer payments were removed, it would be next to impossible for Canada to establish new national programs. Reduced funding for women's advocacy and research weakened the equality impetus; feminist activism in the area of legislative reforms and equality policies underwent a decline.

Lee Lakeman, a founder of one of Canada's first shelters for women in violent relationships, described the shift in government: "Government vocabulary changed — they spoke less about 'the community' and more about 'the stakeholders,' and government intervention came less to protect 'human rights' and more to protect 'corporate rights'. The discourse had changed on every basic value. Social services were suddenly 'luxuries.'"[2]

Canada did not create a national daycare program at this time, but provincial and territorial governments entered separate funding agreements with the Ottawa to develop daycare at the provincial level. Standards for care provided and rates of pay for daycare workers varied from province to province, as did the level of subsidies provided to daycare spaces by governments to make quality care affordable. As a result, daycare fees ranged from as little as $5 a day in Quebec to $50 a day in Ontario. And, according to the *Status of Day Care in Canada in 1995 and 1996*, fewer than 50 percent of children whose parents were employed or studying had access to licensed daycare. The number of licensed spaces in Canada in 1995 was 516,734.

Nora Spinks, chief executive officer of the Vanier Institute of the Family, said, "We need to be bold and courageous — to be as forward-thinking as our ancestors were when they made a commitment to publicly funding education in this country." Meanwhile, economists calculated that investing $1 million in childcare creates forty jobs — four times as many jobs as generated by the same level of investment as construction spending.

Globally, structural adjustment programs were being imposed on poorer countries due to pressure by the World Bank and the International Monetary Fund. Within this climate, even well-off countries like Canada curbed public spending under the guise of debt reduction, and at the same time reduced the corporate tax burden. As governments placed less of a priority to improving the quality of life of their citizens, women's political voices became less authoritative than those of bankers and businessmen.

In Quebec, concerns about the poverty of women and Aboriginal people formed the backdrop for a historic Bread and Roses March in May 1995, organized by the Fédération des femmes du Québec. Some eight hundred marchers walked for ten days and covered 200 km. The march culminated at the Quebec National Assembly on June 4 in Quebec City where they were met by fifteen thousand supporters. The march led to important victories for women in Quebec that included pay equity, a raise in the minimum wage and a reduction of the sponsorship period from ten years to three years for immigrant women sponsored by their spouse. The federation's president Françoise David went on to help organize a World March of Women in 2000, a global initiative involving approximately five thousand organizations from 159 countries and territories. David spoke at the United Nations about the rages of war and the impact of neoliberal policies on women around the world.

Women still made up a disproportionate proportion of the poor in Canada, 2.4 million compared to 1.9 million men. In particular, the poverty rate for senior women at the end of the twentieth century was 19.3 percent while that of senior men was 9.5 percent, according to Statistics Canada. Thirty-six percent of Aboriginal

Canada's Murdered Aboriginal Women

Between 1980 and 2012, there were 1,017 Aboriginal female victims of homicide in Canada, which represents roughly 16% of all female homicides – far greater than their 4% representation in Canada's female population.

Source: RCMP; Statistics Canada. All values approximate.

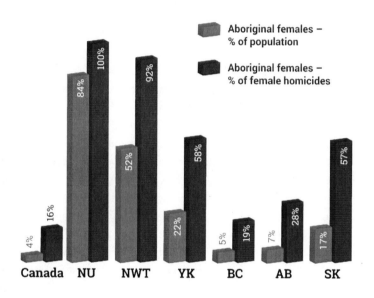

Aboriginal females –
% of population

Aboriginal females –
% of female homicides

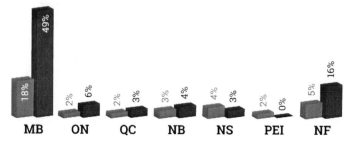

women in Canada lived in poverty, as did 23 percent of immigrant women. Just over half of single-parent households headed by women were living in poverty. Just over half of Aboriginal women were in the labour force at this time. The rate of unemployment for Aboriginal women was 13.5 percent, compared to 6.4 percent for non-Aboriginal women, according to Statistics Canada. Women with disabilities were also less likely to be employed than women without disabilities — just 40 percent of women with disabilities were in the paid workforce.

The legacy of colonialism continued to have distinct effects upon Aboriginal women, who continued to suffer higher rates of violence than non-Aboriginal Women. According to Statistics Canada, Aboriginal women aged fifteen and older were 3.5 times more likely to experience violence than non-Aboriginal women, while rates of spousal assault against Aboriginal women were more than three times higher than those against non-Aboriginal women.

Thirty years after the opening of the first shelters for women in violent relationships, 448 shelters and transition houses were operating. Federal, provincial and municipal governments were spending close to $150 million annually on women's transition homes and emergency shelters, according to Statistics Canada. Some 96,359 women and children stayed in shelters in 1999–2000.

Violence continued to exact its toll, not just on women and children, but on the public purse. Domestic violence, or wife abuse, accounted for an estimated 25 percent of all police-reported violent crime in Canada. The federal Justice Department calculated the total cost of this violence as $7.4 billion a year. It pegged the cost of sexual assault to be $1.9 billion annually. According to researcher Kate McInturff of the Canadian Centre for Policy Alternatives, these calculations are based on estimates of the direct costs in medical and social services, court costs and lost income, as well as estimates of the indirect costs of pain and suffering.[3]

For Aboriginal families, the state often represents a threat to security. Child welfare authorities continued to seize a disproportionate number of Aboriginal children from mothers with a low socio-economic status at the end of the century. "The compromised socioeconomic status of Aboriginal mothers places them in perpetual risk of state intervention; they live their lives in a society that essentially makes poverty a 'quasi' crime and Aboriginal ethnicity a risk factor."[4] The 1996 Royal Commission on Aboriginal People acknowledged that Euro-Western values and beliefs that are reflected in social work practice "are the source reasons for the devastating mass removals of Aboriginal children and their placement in predominantly non-Aboriginal homes."[5] Randi Cull, in her chapter, "Aboriginal Mothering Under the State's Gaze," in *Until Our Hearts Are on the Ground: Aboriginal Mothering, Oppression, Resistance and Rebirth*, writes that fewer than 1 percent of children in state care were Aboriginal in 1955, but by 1969 the figure jumped to 40 percent. The removal of Aboriginal children from their homes and communities continued to be linked to high suicide rates, sexual exploitation, substance use and abuse, poverty and high unemployment.

A WOMAN'S WORK IS NEVER DONE

The issues defined by feminists early in the twentieth century marked women's ongoing equality efforts at the century's close. The participation of women in public life, child welfare, care of the poor and improved working conditions all dominated the feminist landscape of the twentieth century. Strides were made, yet equality remained elusive.

Significant legal gains were won using the rights guarantees in the

Charter. Many people who successfully launched Charter challenges had their cases funded through the Court Challenges Program, a federal program that provided financial and legal support to Charter interest groups to bring forward Charter challenges. The federal government wound down its financial support for the program.[6]

In two precedent-setting Charter cases in 1989, discrimination based on pregnancy, in Brooks *v.* Canada Safeway, and sexual harassment, in Janzen *v.* Platy, were recognized as sex discrimination. In 1997, Robin Eldridge, a deaf B.C. woman, successfully argued that the elimination of public funding for sign language interpretation in B.C. hospitals violated her equal right to medicare. Women and girls also gained more protection in court when testifying against perpetrators of sexual assault. In 1999, in the case of R. *v.* Mills, the Supreme Court limited the circumstances under which those accused of sexual assault could use the personal therapy records of complainants in court. In 1999, the Supreme Court determined in the case of M *v.* H that the exclusion of same-sex couples from the definition of common-law spouse under the Ontario Family Law Act was in violation of equality rights under section 15 of the Charter. The court ruled that the lesbian partners, known as M. and H., had the same financial obligation to each other as heterosexual common-law partners upon separation. The ruling would help lay the groundwork for the legalization of same-sex marriage in 2005.

The participation of women in the workforce continued to be a significant measure of women's economic status at the close of the twentieth century. In 1999, the rate of employment among Canadian women aged twenty-five to fifty-four was 58.9 percent, compared to 66 percent for men. The number of single-parent families led by women had increased, from 377,000 in 1971 to 786,000 in 1991. Overall, however, women were paid just 72.5 cents for every dollar

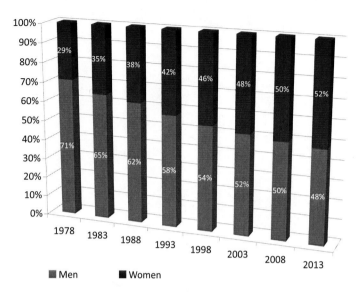

Women's and Men's Union Participation in Canada, 1978–2013
Statistics Canada, 2013. Labour force survey estimates (LFS), employees by union coverage, North American Industry Classification System (NAICS), sex and age group. CANSIM. Table 282-0078.

earned by men doing similar work and with similar education.[7] Women most likely to see the smallest wage gap (89 percent) were those in medicine, dentistry, veterinary medicine and optometry. Almost the same proportion of the female workforce (32 percent) as the male workforce (34 percent) held unionized jobs at the turn of the twenty-first century. Women accounted for 46 percent of the workforce at the end of the century, up from 37.1 percent in 1976. According to Statistics Canada, two thirds of all employed women at this time worked in teaching, nursing, health, clerical, sales and service occupations. As well, 60 percent of women with children under age three were in the workforce, nearly double the percentage who worked for wages in 1976.[8]

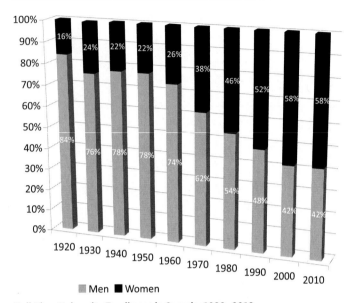

Full-Time University Enrollment in Canada, 1920–2012
Source: Equality in Employment: A Royal Commission Report by Rosalie Siberman Abella, (1984) and
Statistics Canada.

The rise in the education level of women one hundred years after they were first admitted to universities represents another important marker. In 1970, 38 percent of of those enrolled full-time in undergraduate programs were women. By the turn of the century, women made up 58 percent — a number that holds steady today.

Women slowly increased their representation in many professional fields. Half of those employed in both diagnostic and treating positions in medicine and related health professions and in business and financial professional positions were women at the turn of the century. Women also nearly doubled their participation rate in building construction trades, electronics and electricity from 1.25 percent in 1990, to 2.4 percent in 2000.

Politics continued to be an important stage on which women's equality played out. Of the 301 seats in the House of Commons in 1997, 20.6 percent (sixty-two seats) were held by women. In the Senate, 22 of 105 seats were occupied by women seven decades after the Persons Case. Sandra Lovelace, who brought the cause of discrimination of women in the Indian Act to the United Nations in 1979, would be the first Aboriginal woman appointed to the Canadian Senate, in 2004. Television broadcaster Adrienne Clarkson, in 1999, became the first person of colour to be appointed governor general.

The first female premier in Canada, Rita Johnston, served as premier of B.C. for seven months after being elected leader of the province's Social Credit Party in 1991. In P.E.I., Catherine Callbeck became the first woman to be elected premier, in 1993. Pat Duncan was elected premier of the Yukon in 2000.

A gender gap in federal voting patterns confirms that female voters continue to be much more likely than male voters to support parties with an emphasis on social programs, while men are more likely to prioritize debt reduction and tax cuts. As such, a significantly higher percentage of male voters compared to female voters support conservative parties and a slightly higher percentage of female voters support the Liberals, NDP and the Bloc Québécois. Liberal caucuses tend to have a higher percentage of women compared to those of conservative parties. Under the leadership of the federal NDP's second female leader, Alexa McDonough, the party's caucus was 30 percent female after the 1997 election.

Meanwhile in the nation's boardrooms, women made up fewer than 10 percent of corporate directors on Canada's five hundred largest company boards in 2000. Slightly more than half of corporate boards at this time were all male; however, the representation of women directors increased in the next decade to 17 percent.

Unquestionably, the women's movement had a profound effect on all elements of Canadian society. The movement and the relentless courage of its leaders brought about nothing less than a restructuring of society, a revolution that changed the way we think about gender roles, child rearing, sexuality and marriage. In the public domain, women's efforts beginning in the early twentieth century were instrumental to the formation of the social safety net. And while that net grew between 1920 and 1980, it ceased to expand significantly by the end of the century.

"By stressing that 'the personal is political,' the women's movement has made the social inequality of women a public and not merely a private problem," concluded feminist researchers Margrit Eichler and Marie Lavigne in the *Canadian Encyclopedia*. "This accomplishment is its single most important contribution."[9]

Women have not only achieved equality "rights," but have also shifted our understanding of power and leadership, our beliefs about science, including psychology, and, through their activist efforts, our beliefs about the duty of care we have to preserve the environment. The women's movement has compelled governments, courts, the media, businesses, unions, law enforcement agencies, professional associations and religious institutions to be more diverse and less tolerant of discrimination. In so doing, women have changed the fabric of society and its values, as well as the destiny of its citizens. Women's efforts created new programs, improved laws and greater equality for marginalized groups.

Although women's equality was not fully achieved by the end of the twentieth century, new generations of women, picking up where their foremothers left off, continue to sharpen the tools of feminism, fight injustice and forge alliances to imagine a better country and make a better world.

NOTES

CHAPTER 1: FROM BLUESTOCKINGS TO BRA-BURNERS

1. Joan Wallach Scott, 1996, *Only Paradoxes to Offer: French Feminists and the Rights of Man,* Cambridge, MA: Harvard University Press, p.52.
2. Maria, 1782, "To the Editor of the Gazetteer," *Gazetteer and New Daily Advertiser,* January 23, 1782, London, p.2.
3. Mary Wollstonecraft, originally published in 1792, *Vindication of the Rights of Woman,* London, U.K.: Penguin, p.81.
4. Rose Tremain, 1975, *The Fight for Freedom for Women,* New York: Ballantine Books.

Chapter 2: First Nations Women

1. Randi Cull, 2006, "Aboriginal Mothering Under the State's Gaze," in D. Memme Lavell-Harvard and Jeannette Corbiere Lavell (eds.), *Until Our Hearts Are on the Ground: Aboriginal Mothering, Oppression, Resistance and Rebirth,* Toronto: Demeter Press, p.143.
2. Patricia D. McGuire and Patricia A. Monture, (eds.), 2009, *First Voices: An Aboriginal Women's Reader,* Toronto: Inanna Publications, pp.68–69.
3. Cyndy Baskin, 2006, "Women in Iroquois Society," *Canadian Woman Studies Journal,* Vol. 4, Issue 2, Toronto: Inanna Publications and

Education, pp.42–46.

4. Jan Noel, 2006, "Power Mothering: The Haudenosaunee Model," in D. Memme Lavell-Harvard and Jeannette Corbiere Lavell (eds.), *Until Our Hearts Are on the Ground: Aboriginal Mothering, Oppression, Resistance and Rebirth,* Toronto: Demeter Press, p.79.

5. Kim Anderson, 2000, *A Recognition of Being: Reconstructing Native Womanhood,* Toronto: Second Story Press.

6. Barbara Alice Mann, 2004, *Iroquoian Women: The Gantowisas,* New York: Peter Lang.

7. Merna Forster, 2004, *100 Canadian Heroines: Famous and Forgotten Faces,* Toronto: The Dundurn Group, p.255.

8. Mona Holmlund and Gail Youngberg (eds.), 2003, *Inspiring Women: A Celebration of Herstory,* Regina: Coteau Books, p.41.

9. Jean Barman, 2011, "Indigenous Women on the Cusp of Contact," in Cheryl Suzack, Shari M. Huhndorf, Jeanne Perreault and Jean Barman (eds.), *Indigenous Women and Feminism: Politics, Activism, Culture,* Vancouver: UBC Press, p.97.

10. James Strange, 1982, *James Strange's Journal and Narrative,* Fairfield, WA: Ye Galleon Press, p.84, as quoted in Jean Barman, 2011, "Indigenous Women on the Cusp of Contact," p.98.

11. Jean Barman, 2011, "Indigenous Women on the Cusp of Contact," p.98.

12. Merna Forster, 2004, *100 Canadian Heroines,* p.179.

13. Jan Noel, 2006, *Until Our Hearts Are on the Ground,* p.86.

14. Lina Sunseri, 2009, "Moving Beyond the Feminism Versus the Nationalism Dichotomy," in Patricia A. Monture and Patricia D. McGuire (eds.), *First Voices: An Aboriginal Women's Reader,* Toronto: Inanna Publications, p.258.

15. Sharon D. McIvor, 2009, "Aboriginal Women's Rights as 'Existing Rights,'" in Patricia A. Monture and Patricia D. McGuire (eds.), *First Voices: An Aboriginal Women's Reader,* Toronto: Inanna Publications, p.375.

16. Rene R. Gadacz, 2013, "Potlatch," *Canadian Encyclopedia,* <http://thecanadianencyclopedia.com>.

17. Sarah Carter, 2008, *The Importance of Being Monogamous: Marriage and Nation Building in Western Canada to 1915*, Edmonton: University of Alberta Press, p.10.

18. C. Bourassa, K. McKay-McNabb and M. Hampton, 2009, "Racism, Sexism and Colonialism: The Impact on the Health of Aboriginal Women in Canada" in Patricia A. Monture and Patricia D. McGuire (eds.), *First Voices: An Aboriginal Women's Reader*, Toronto: Inanna Publications, p.297.

CHAPTER 3: COLONIAL WOMEN, 1630–1850

1. Linda Rasmussen, Lorna Rasmussen, Candace Savage, Anne Wheeler, 1976, *A Harvest Yet to Reap: A History of Prairie Women,* Toronto: Women's Press, p.12.

2. Mona Holmlund and Gail Youngberg (eds.), 2003, *Inspiring Women,* p.4.

3. Mona Holmlund and Gail Youngberg (eds.), 2003, *Inspiring Women,* p.6.

4. Mona Holmlund and Gail Youngberg (eds.), 2003, *Inspiring Women,* p.7.

5. Tom Derreck, 2002, "Soldier Girl: The Emma Edmonds Story," *Beaver*, September, Winnipeg, pp.26–31.

6. Merna Forster, 2004, *100 Canadian Heroines,* pp.40–42.

7. Sarah Grimke, 1838, *Letters on the Equality of the Sexes and the Condition of Woman*, Boston, MA: I. Knapp.

8. Declaration of Sentiments and Resolutions, 1840, *Report of the Woman's Rights Convention held at Seneca Falls, New York July 19 and July 20, 1840.*

9. Sojourner Truth, 1851, Address to women's convention, Acron, Ohio, December.

10. Joseph Mensah, 2010. *Black Canadians*, Halifax: Fernwood.

11. Alison Prentice, Paula Bourne, Gail Cuthbert Brandt, Beth Light, Wendy Mitchinson, Naomi Black, 1988, *Canadian Women: A History,* Toronto: Harcourt Brace Jovanovich, p.57.

12. Constance Backhouse, 1999, *Colour Coded: A Legal History of Racism in Canada 1900–1950,* Toronto: University of Toronto Press, p.257.

13. Virtual Museum of Canada, 2007, "New Brunswick: Our Stories: Our People," January 31 <http://www.gnb.ca/cnb/news/wcs/2007e0118wc.htm>.

14. Lawrence Hill, 2010, *The Book of Negroes,* Toronto: Harper Collins, p.472.

15. Rosemary Sadlier, 2012, *Harriet Tubman: Freedom Seeker, Freedom Leader,* Toronto: Dundurn, p.113.

16. Merna Forster, 2004, *100 Canadian Heroines.*

17. Heather Murray, 2002, *Come, Bright Improvement! The Literary Societies of Nineteenth-Century Ontario,* Toronto: University of Toronto Press, p.71.

18. Prentice, Bourne, Cuthbert et al., 1988, *Canadian Women,* p.175.

19. Heather Murray, 2002, *Come, Bright Improvement,* p.107.

CHAPTER 4: WOMEN AT CONFEDERATION, 1870–1899

1. Jeanne L'Espérance, 1982, *The Widening Sphere: Women in Canada, 1870–1940,* Ottawa: Public Archives Canada, p.23.

2. Prentice, Bourne, Cuthbert et al., 1988, *Canadian Women,* p.174.

3. Philip Girard with Jim Philips, 2011, "Rethinking 'the Nation' in National Legal History: A Canadian Perspective," *Law and History Review,* Cambridge: Cambridge University Press.

4. Sarah Carter, 2008, *The Importance of Being Monogamous,* p.282.

5. Prentice, Bourne, Cuthbert et al., 1988, *Canadian Women,* p.89.

6. Sarah Carter, 2008, *The Importance of Being Monogamous,* p.25.

7. Jeanne L'Espérance, 1982, *The Widening Sphere,* p.38.

8. Merna Forster, 2004, *100 Canadian Heroines,* p.311.

9. *Canadian Encyclopedia Volume III,* 1985, Edmonton: Hurtig Publishers, p.1763.

10. Beverley Boutilier, 1997, *Creating Historical Memory: English Canadian Women and the Work of History,* Beverly Boutilier and Alison Prentice (eds.), Vancouver: UBC Press.

11. Prentice, Bourne, Cuthbert et al., 1988, *Canadian Women,* p.178.

12. Prentice, Bourne, Cuthbert et al., 1988, *Canadian Women,* p.179.

13. Government of Canada, 2010, Parks Canada Backgrounder, "Women's Christian Temperance Union," Ottawa <www.pc.gc.ca/APPS/CP-NR/release_e.asp?bgid=114&andor1=bg>.

14. Harry Gutkin and Mildred Gutkin, 1996, "How the Vote Was Won," *Manitoba History*, Autumn, Winnipeg: The Manitoba Historical Society.

15. N.E.S. Griffiths, 1993, *The Splendid Vision: Centennial History of the National Council of Women of Canada 1893–1993,* Ottawa: Carleton University Press, p.6.

16. N.E.S. Griffiths, 1993, *The Splendid Vision,* p.10.

17. N.E.S. Griffiths, 1993, *The Splendid Vision,* p.21.

18. Merna Forster, 2004, *100 Canadian Heroines,* p.24.

19. Prentice, Bourne, Cuthbert et al., 1988 *Canadian Women,* p.183.

20. N.E.S. Griffiths, 1993, *The Splendid Vision,* p.5.

21. Manon Tremblay, 2010, *Quebec Women and Legislative Representation,* Vancouver: UBC Press, p.12.

22. Elections Canada, Women and Political Participation in Canada, n.d., <elections.ca/res/eim/article_search/article.asp?id=84&lang=e&frmPageSize=>.

23. Canadian citizenship was not created until the Canadian Citizenship Act, 1946, which came into effect on January 1, 1947. Until then, immigrants who lived in Canada for a specified period, and people born in Canada, were legally referred to as British subjects.

24. Elections Canada, A History of the Vote in Canada, Chapter 2 <www.elections.ca/content.aspx?section=res&dir=his&document=chap2&lang=e#a27 Elections Canada online>.

25. Prentice, Bourne, Cuthbert et al., 1988 *Canadian Women,* p.176.

26. Micheline Dumont, 2012, *Feminism à la Québécoise,* Toronto: Feminist Historical Society, p.26.

27. Prentice, Bourne, Cuthbert et al., 1988 *Canadian Women,* p.115.

28 Henry Gutkin and Mildrid Gutkin, 1996, "How the Manitoba Vote Was Won," *Manitoba History* No. 32 (Autumn), Winnipeg: Manitoba

Historical Society.

29. Prentice, Bourne, Cuthbert et al., 1988 *Canadian Women,* p.186.

30. Jeanne L'Esperance, 1982, *The Widening Sphere,* p.7.

31. Jeanne L'Esperance, 1982, *The Widening Sphere,* p.25.

32. Prentice, Bourne, Cuthbert et al., 1988 *Canadian Women,* p.125.

33. Janice Newton, 1995, *The Feminist Challenge to the Canadian Left 1900–1918,* McGill Queens University Press, p.92.

34. Prentice, Bourne, Cuthbert et al., 1988 *Canadian Women,* p.125.

35. Jeanne L'Espérance, 1982, *The Widening Sphere,* p.25.

36. Jaques Ferland, 1986, "When the Cotton Mills 'Girls' Struck for the First Time: A Study of Female Militancy in the Cotton and Shoe Factories of Quebec (1880–1910)," paper presented to the Canadian Historical Association, Winnipeg, pp 18–19.

37. Gregory S. Kealey, 1980, *Toronto Workers Respond to Industrial Capitalism, 1867–1892,* Toronto: University of Toronto Press, p.50.

38. Gregory S. Kealey, 1980, *Toronto Workers Respond.*

39. Gregory S. Kealey, 2003. "McVICAR, Kate," in *Dictionary of Canadian Biography,* vol. 11, University of Toronto/Université Laval <www.biographi.ca/en/bio/mcvicar_kate_11E.html>.

40. Ruth A. Frager and Carmela Patrias, 2005, *Discounted Labour: Women Workers in Canada, 1870–1939,* Toronto: University of Toronto Press, p.105.

41. Prentice, Bourne, Cuthbert et al., 1988 *Canadian Women,* p.127.

42. Mona Holmlund and Gail Youngberg (eds.), 2003, *Inspiring Women,* p.132.

43. Susan E. Merritt, 1995, *Her Story II*: Women from Canada's Past, St. Catherines: Vanwell Publishing.

44. Mona Holmlund and Gail Youngberg (eds.), 2003, *Inspiring Women,* p.142.

45. Frances Backhouse, 1995, *Women of the Klondike,* Vancouver: Whitecap Books, p.161.

46. Bay Ryley, 1997, *Gold Diggers of the Klondike,* Winnipeg: Watson and Dwyer.

47. Micheline Dumont, 2012, *Feminism à la Québécoise,* p.20.

48. Merna Forster, 2004, *100 Canadian Heroines,* p.67–69.

49. Susan J. Johnston, 2003, "Hussey, Florence Sarah," in *Dictionary of Canadian Biography*, vol. 14, University of Toronto/Université Laval <http://www.biographi.ca/en/bio.php?id_nbr=7461>.

50. Susan Jackel, 1987, "First Days, Fighting Days: Prairie Presswomen and Suffrage Activism, 1906–1916," in Mary Kinnear (ed.), *First Days, Fighting Days: Women in Manitoba History,* University of Regina Canadian Plains Research Centre.

CHAPTER 5: THE SUFFRAGE ERA, 1900–1919

1. Veronica Strong-Boag and Carole Gerson, 2000, *Paddling Her Own Canoe: The Times and Texts of E. Pauline Johnson Tekahionwake,* Toronto: University of Toronto Press, p.59.

2. Linda Kay, 2013, *Sweet Sixteen: The Journey That Inspired the Canadian Women's Press Club,* Montreal, McGill Queen's University Press, p.12.

3. Debbie Marshall, 2007, *Give Your Other Vote to the Sister,* Calgary: University of Calgary Press.

4. Linda Rasmussen, Lorna Rasmussen, Candace Savage and Anne Wheeler, 1976, *A Harvest Yet to Reap,* Women's Press, p.123.

5. Manitoba Historical Society, 2009, "Timelines: Francis Marion Beynon" <http://www.mhs.mb.ca/docs/features/timelinks/reference/db0006.shtml>.

6. Ruth A. Frager and Carmela Patrias, 2005, *Discounted Labour,* p.46.

7. Ruth A. Frager and Carmela Patrias, 2005, *Discounted Labour,* 2005.

8. Joan Sangster, *Canadian Encyclopedia,* Volume III, p.1959.

9. Mona Holmlund and Gail Youngberg (eds.), 2003, *Inspiring Women,* p.173.

10. Mona Holmlund and Gail Youngberg (eds.), 2003, *Inspiring Women,* p.133.

11. Prentice, Bourne, Cuthbert et al., 1988 *Canadian Women,* p.114.

12. Micheline Dumont, 2012, *Feminism à la Québécoise,* p.28.

13. Micheline Dumont, 2012, *Feminism à la Québécoise,* p.29.

14. Prentice, Bourne, Cuthbert et al., 1988 *Canadian Women,* p.203.

15. Merna Forster, 2004, *100 Canadian Heroines,* p.169.

16. Jeanne L'Espérance, 1982, *The Widening Sphere,* p.53.

17. Mona Holmlund and Gail Youngberg (eds.), 2003, *Inspiring Women,* p.151.

18. Debbie Marshall, 2007, *Give Your Other Vote to the Sister,* pp.102–104.

19. Mary Hallett and Marilyn Davis, 1993, *Firing the Heather: The Life and Times of Nellie McClung,* Saskatoon: Fifth House Publishing, p.151.

20. Candace Savage, 1979, *Our Nell: A Scrapbook Biography of Nellie L. McClung,* Saskatoon: Western Producer Prairie Books.

21. Mary Hallett and Marilyn Davis, 1993, *Firing the Heather,* p.151.

22. N.E.S. Griffiths, 1993, *The Splendid Vision,* p.140.

23. Sharon Carstairs and Tim Higgins, 2004, *Dancing Backwards: A Social History of Canadian Women in Politics,* Winnipeg: Heartland.

24. Candace Savage, 1979, *Our Nelle, A Scrapbook Biography of Nellie L. McClung,* Saskatoon: Western Producer Prairie Books.

25. Mildred Gutkin and Harry Gutkin, 2007, *Profiles in Dissent: The Shaping of Political Thought in the Canadian West,* Regina: NeWest Press.

26. Daniel Francis, 2007, Seeing *Reds: The Red Scare of 1918–1919, Canada's First War on Terror,* Toronto: Arsenal Pulp Press, p.201.

CHAPTER 6: THE INTER-WAR YEARS, 1920–1939

1. Micheline Dumont, 2012, *Feminism à la Québécoise,* p.34.

2. Daniel Francis, 2007, *Seeing Reds.*

3. Status of Women Canada, 2000, *Making History, Building Futures: Women of the 20th Century,* brochure, n.d., Ottawa.

4. N.E.S. Griffiths, 1993, *The Splendid Vision,* p.229.

5. N.E.S. Griffiths, 1993, *The Splendid Vision,* p.18.

6. Mona Holmlund and Gail Youngberg (eds.), 2003, *Inspiring Women,* p.106.

7. Sharon Carstairs and Tim Higgins, 2004, *Dancing Backwards,* p.71.

8. Micheline Dumont, 2012, *Feminism à la Québécoise,* p.57.

9. Robert J. Sharpe and Patricia I. McMahon, 2007, *The Persons Case:*

The Origins and Legacy of the Fight for Legal Personhood, University of Toronto Press.

10. James H. Marsh, 2012, "Eugenics," *Canadian Encyclopedia* <www. thecanadianencyclopedia.ccom>.

11. Sharon Carstairs and Tim Higgins, 2004, *Dancing Backwards,* p.155.

12. Prentice, Bourne, Cuthbert et al., 1988 *Canadian Women,* p.235.

13. Andrée Lévesque, 1994, *Making and Breaking the Rules: Women in Quebec 1919–1939* (translation by Yvonne M, Klein), Toronto: University of Toronto Press, p.51.

14. Ruth A. Frager and Carmela Patrias, 2005, *Discounted Labour,* p.45.

15. Andrée Lévesque, 1994, *Making and Breaking the Rules,* p.84.

16. Angus McLaren, 1991, "Keep Your Seats and Face Facts: Western Canadian Women's Discussion of Birth Control," *Canadian Bulletin of Medical History* Volume 8: Waterloo, Wilfrid Laurier University Press, p.195.

17. *Western Producer,* 1927, 24 February, p.12.

18. Mona Holmlund and Gail Youngberg (eds.), 2003, *Inspiring Women,* p.102.

19. Merna Forster, 2004, *100 Canadian Heroines,* p.44.

20. Toronto: Doubleday Canada, p.40.

21. Andrée Lévesque, 1994, *Making and Breaking the Rules,* p.102.

CHAPTER 7: THE SECOND WORLD WAR ERA, 1940–1959

1. N.E.S. Griffiths, 1993, *The Splendid Vision,* p.212.

2. Roach Pierson, 1986, *They're Still Women After All: The Second World War and Canadian Womanhood,* Toronto: McClelland and Stewart, p.61.

3. Roach Pierson, 1986, *They're Still Women,* p.57.

4. Merna Forster, 2004, *100 Canadian Heroines,* p.143.

5. Roach Pierson, 1986, *They're Still Women,* p 113.

6. Ruth Russell (ed.), 2006, *Proudly She Marched, Training Canada's World War II Women in Waterloo County,* Volume 1: Canadian Women's Army Corps, p.8.

7. Roach Pierson, 1986, *They're Still Women,* p.135.

8. Roach Pierson, 1986, *They're Still Women,* p.190.

9. Roach Pierson, 1986, *They're Still Women,* pp.188–95.

10. Midge Ayukawa, 2004, "Japanese Pioneer Women," in Marlene Epp, Franca Jacovetta and Frances Swyripa (eds.), *Sisters or Strangers: Immigrant, Ethnic, and Racialized Women in Canadian History,* Toronto: University of Toronto Press, p.237.

11. Merna Forster, 2011, *100 More Canadian Heroines: Famous and Forgotten Faces,* Toronto: The Dundurn Group, p.205.

12. Roach Pierson, 1986, *They're Still Women,* p.82.

13. N.E.S. Griffiths, 1993, *The Splendid Vision,* pp.229–35.

14. Merna Forster, 2011, *100 More Canadian Heroines,* p.257.

15. Pat Connelly, with Marilyn Keddy, 1989, "Interview With Madeleine Parent," *Studies in Political Economy* 30, Autumn, p.13.

16. Dean Jobb, 2009, "Ticket to Freedom," *Beaver,* April–May.

CHAPTER 8: THE WOMEN'S LIBERATION MOVEMENT, 1960–1999

1. Lisa Rundle, 2006, "Still Ain't Satisfied," *Herizons,* Winter, Winnipeg.

2. Penney Kome, 1985, *Women of Influence,* p.70.

3. Status of Women Canada 2000, n.d. "Making History Building Futures: Women of the 20th Century," brochure, Ottawa.

4. Judy Rebick (ed.), 2005, *Ten Thousand Roses: The Making of a Feminist Revolution,* Toronto: Penguin, p.57.

5. Constance Backhouse and David H. Flaherty (eds.), 1992, *Challenging Times: The Women's Movement in Canada and the United States,* McGill-Queens University Press, p.19.

6. Marion Douglas Kerans, 1996, *Muriel Duckworth: A Very Active Pacifist,* Halifax: Fernwood Publishing, p.90.

7. Prentice, Bourne, Cuthbert et al., 1988 *Canadian Women,* p.336.

8. Anna Holmes, 2011, "Spotlighting the Work of Women in the Civil Rights Movement's Freedom Rides," *Washington Post,* June 2.

9. Monique Begin, 1992, "The Royal Commission on the Status of Women," in Constance Backhouse and David H. Flaherty (eds.),

Challenging Times, the Women's Movement in Canada and the United States, Montreal: McGill Queen's University Press.

10. Prentice, Bourne, Cuthbert et al., 1988 *Canadian Women,* p.406.

11. Louise Arbour, 1996, *Commission of Inquiry into Certain Events at The Prison for Women in Kingston,* Ottawa: Public Works and Government Services Canada, p.9.

12. Pamela Cross, 2000, "Report of the Royal Commission on the Status of Women: Where Are We After Thirty Years?" Ontario Women's Justice Network, November <http://owjn.org/owjn_2009/legal-information/aboriginal-law/197#ab>.

13. Lisa Young, 1998, "The Canadian Women's Movement and Political Parties, 1970–1993," In Manon Tremblay and Caroline Andrew (eds.), *Women and Political Representation in Canada,* University of Ottawa Press, pp.204–11.

14. Agnes Huang and Fatima Jaffer, 1993, "Interview with Judy Rebick," *Kinesis,* June, Vancouver, pp.10–11.

15. Johanna Brand, 1993, "Making Our Vote Count," *Herizons,* 7, 3, (Fall), p.19.

16. Susan Judith Ship, 1998, "Problematizing Ethnicity and Race in Feminist Scholarship on Women and Politics," in Caroline Andrew and Manon Tremblay (eds.), *Women and Political Representation in Canada,* Ottawa: University of Ottawa Press, p.328.

17. Penni Mitchell, 1993, "Time for Change: Will A.M. Be our Next P.M.?" *Herizons,* 7, 1 (Spring), Winnipeg.

18. Lyn Cockburn, 2010, "And Justice for All," *Herizons,* 24, 1 (Summer), Winnipeg.

19. Lyn Cockburn, 2010, "And Justice for All."

20. Johanna Brand, 1993, "Making Our Vote Count."

21. Manon Tremblay, 2001, "Women and Political Representation in Canada," Elections Canada Electoral Insight <www.elections.ca/res/eim/article_search/article.asp?id=84&lang=e&frmPageSize>.

22. *Report of the Task force on Child Care,* 1986, Ottawa: Government of Canada, p.333.

23. Judy LaMarsh, 1968, *Memoirs of a Bird in a Gilded Cage,* Toronto:

McClelland and Stewart.

24. Marilou McPhedran and Susan Basilli, 2009, "Women's Constitutional Activism in Canada and South Africa," The International Review of Constitutionalism 9: 02, Florida: Book World Publications.

25. Claire L'Heureux-Dubé, 2010, "Preface," in Kim Brooks (ed.), *Justice Bertha Wilson*, Vancouver: UBC Press, p.x.

26. Judy Rebick (ed.), 2005, *Ten Thousand Roses.*

27. Judy Rebick (ed.), 2005, *Ten Thousand Roses,* p.41.

28. Kathryn Keate, 1970, *Toronto Women's Liberation Newsletter,* June 22, pp.6–7, as cited in "The Politics of the Body," 1993, in Ruth Roach Pearson, Marjorie Griffin Cohen, Paula Bourne, Philanda Masters (eds.), *Canadian Women's Issues Volume 1: Strong Voices,* Toronto: James Lorimer and Company, pp.126–27.

29. Amanda LeRougetel, 2009, "Norma Scarborough's Legacy Lives On," *Herizons,* 23, 1 (Summer), Winnipeg.

30. Holly Johnson, 2008, "Foreword," in Jane Ursel, Leslie M. Tutty, Janice leMaistre (eds.), *What's Law Got to Do With It? The Law, Specialized Courts and Domestic Violence in Canada,* Toronto: Cormorant Books, p.ix.

31. Nancy Janovicek, 2007, *No Place to Go, Local Histories of the Battered Women's Movement,* Vancouver: UBC Press, p.6.

32. Jane Ursel, Leslie M. Tutty and Janice leMaistre, 2008, "The Justice System Response to Domestic Violence: Debates, Discussions and Dialogues," in Jane Ursel, Leslie M. Tutty and Janice leMaistre (eds.), *What's Law Got to Do With It? The Law, Specialized Courts and Domestic Violence in Canada,* Toronto: Cormorant Books, p.1.

33. Changing the Landscape: Ending Violence, Achieving Equality, Executive Summary/National Action Plan, 1991, The Canadian Panel on Violence Against Women, Ottawa, Minister of Supply and Services Canada, p.11.

34. Department of Justice, 2012, *A Handbook for Police and Crown Prosecutors on Criminal Harassment,* Ottawa: Public Works and Government Services Canada.

35. Richard Jochelson and Kirsten Kramar, 2011, *Sex and the Supreme Court: Obscenity and Indecency Laws in Canada*, Halifax: Fernwood Publishing, p.37.

36. Jochelson and Kramar, 2011, *Sex and the Supreme Court*, p.40.

CHAPTER 9: THE END OF THE TWENTIETH CENTURY

1. Shelagh Day, 2010, "Dear Mr. Ignatief," *Herizons*, 23, 3 (Winter), Winnipeg.

2. Lee Lakeman, 2000, "Why Law and Order Won't Stop Violence Against Women," *Herizons*, 14, 2 (Fall), Winnipeg.

3. Kate McInturff, 2013, "Preventing Violence a Good Investment," *Herizons*, 27, 2 (Fall), Winnipeg.

4. Randi Cull, 2006, "Aboriginal Mothering Under the State's Gaze," in D. Memme Lavell-Harvard and Jeannette Corbiere Lavell (eds.), *Until Our Hearts Are on the Ground: Aboriginal Mothering, Oppression, Resistance and Rebirth*, Toronto: Demeter Press, p.147.

5. Randi Cull, 2006, "Aboriginal Mothering," p.146.

6. In 2006, Prime Minister Stephen Harper cancelled the $5.5 million program.

7. Status of Women Canada, n.d., *Making History, Building Futures: Women of the 20th Century*, brochure, Ottawa.

8. Statistics Canada, 2006, *Women in Canada: A Gender-Based Statistical Report*, 5th edition, March, p.13.

9. Margrit Eichler and Marie Lavigne, "Women's Movement," *Canadian Encyclopedia* <http://www.thecanadianencyclopedia.com/articles/womens-movement>.

INDEX